Irvin D. Yalom, emeritus
University, is the auth
bestselling books includi
Therapy, Becoming Myself,
Yalom's books include classics of cultural history such as
A History of the Wife, Birth of the Chess Queen, and *How
the French Invented Love,* as well as her final book released
posthumously, *Innocent Witnesses: Childhood Memories of
World War II.* They were married for sixty-five years.

Praise for *A Matter of Death and Life*

"*A Matter of Death and Life* is wise, beautiful, heartbreaking, raw – a paean to enduring love and what it means."

—*The Times*

"For over half a century, the eminent psychiatrist Irvin Yalom has dazzled the world with his stories of the human psyche packed with wisdom, insight, and humor. Now, with stunning candor and courage, he shares with us the most difficult experience of his life: the loss of his wife and steadfast companion since adolescence. Partners to the end, including in the co-writing of this book, they share an indelible portrait of bereavement—the terror, pain, denial, and reluctant acceptance. But what we are left with is much more than a profound story of enduring loss—it's an unforgettable and achingly beautiful story of enduring love. I will be thinking about this for years to come."

—Lori Gottlieb, *New York Times* bestselling author of
*Maybe You Should Talk to Someone: A Therapist,
Her Therapist, and Our Lives Revealed*

"Marilyn and Irvin write so luminously I feel I have lived that period of time alongside them . . . I was deeply touched by Irvin's humility in acknowledging that we are simply unprepared for the great encounter with death, or for the loss of a soulmate, no matter how closely we observe these stories as professionals. This book is illuminating and vivid, a beautiful examination of the consolation of a life well-lived, and a beacon of hope to all of us who will be bereaved. And of course, it is an exposition of how we who are mortal learn to live with that very truth about ourselves."

—Kathryn Mannix, *Sunday Times* bestselling author of
*With the End in Mind: Dying, Death and
Wisdom in an Age of Denial*

"This beautiful, poignant, and uplifting memoir is a love story, a tale of two incredibly accomplished lives that were lived almost as one, the sum turning out to be so much greater than its parts. It will inspire you and perhaps move you to look differently at your life—it did that for me."

—Abraham Verghese, author of *Cutting for Stone*

"The Yaloms are not just honest, but astonishingly generous with their readers. This book takes its immediate place in the canon of great end-of-life memoirs."

—Caitlin Doughty, founder of The Order of the Good Death

"*A Matter of Death and Life* is both a sweet reminiscence and a path to discovery. Two eminent professors, authors, and lifelong partners grapple with aging, fragility, and death. In the process of honestly meeting the precariousness of life, they come to a deeper appreciation of its preciousness."

—Frank Ostaseski, author of *The Five Invitations: Discovering What Death Can Teach Us About Living Fully*

"*A Matter of Death and Life* is so much more than a book. It is an indefatigable love story. It is a text that traverses past and present. It is exquisite, candid, and vulnerable—absent the too-common defenses of artifice and pomposity—as it approaches the untenable pain of separation and unyielding yearning of loss. Every person would benefit from multiple readings of this intelligently relatable book, both to confront dying as we inch toward our own mortality and, perhaps more importantly, the grief when one so beloved precedes us in death."

—Dr. Joanne Cacciatore, author of *Bearing the Unbearable: Love, Loss, and the Heartbreaking Path of Grief*

"This is a remarkable book—as remarkable as its authors ... *A Matter of Death and Life* is the culmination of the Yaloms' career-long quests for wisdom in the art of living and dying. It is a book that transforms the reader—I couldn't put it down."

—Arthur Kleinman, author of *The Soul of Care: The Moral Education of a Husband and Doctor*

A
MATTER
OF
DEATH
AND
LIFE

Love, Loss and
What Matters in the End

IRVIN D. YALOM AND MARILYN YALOM

PIATKUS

PIATKUS

First published in the United States in 2021 by Redwood Press,
an imprint of Stanford University Press
First published in Great Britain in 2021 by Piatkus
This paperback edition published in 2022 by Piatkus

1 3 5 7 9 10 8 6 4 2

Epigraph by Rabbi Sanford Ragins, originally published in *L'chol Z'man v'Ei: For
Sacred Moments —New Rabbi's Manual*, CCAR Press, © 2015 by Sanford Ragins.
Reprinted with permission.

Excerp⋯ ⋯ *l Poems.*
Co ⋯ /ith
tl ⋯ of

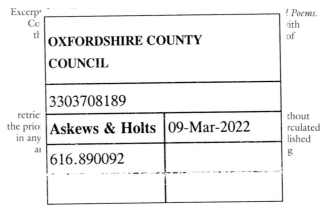

**OXFORDSHIRE COUNTY
COUNCIL**

3303708189	
Askews & Holts	09-Mar-2022
616.890092	

retrie⋯ thout
the prio⋯ rculated
in any⋯ lished
a⋯ g

ISBN 978-0-349-42855-0

Text designed by Kevin Barrett Kane
Printed and bound in Great Britain by Clays Ltd, Elcograf S.p.A.

Papers used by Piatkus are from well-managed forests
and other responsible sources.

Piatkus
An imprint of
Little, Brown Book Group
Carmelite House
50 Victoria Embankment
London EC4Y 0DZ

An Hachette UK Company
www.hachette.co.uk

www.littlebrown.co.uk

*Mourning is the price we pay
for having the courage to love others.*

CONTENTS

CONTENTS

PREFACE

We both embarked on academic careers after postgraduate training at Johns Hopkins, where I had completed a residency in psychiatry and Marilyn obtained a PhD in comparative (French and German) literature. We were always each other's first reader and editor. After I wrote my first book, a textbook on group therapy, I was awarded a writing fellowship from the Rockefeller Foundation at the Bellagio Writing Center in Italy to work on my next book, *Love's Executioner.* Shortly after we arrived, Marilyn spoke to me about her growing interest in writing about women's recollections of the French Revolution, and I agreed that she had ample excellent material for a book. All of the Rockefeller scholars had been given an apartment and a separate writing studio, and I urged her to ask the director whether there might also be a writing studio for her. The director responded that a writing studio for a scholar's spouse was an unusual request and, furthermore, all the studios in the main structure had already been assigned. But, after a few minutes of reflection, he offered Marilyn an unused tree house studio only a five-minute walk away in the adjoining forest. Delighted with it, Marilyn began work, with gusto, on her first book, *Compelled to Witness: Women's Memoirs of the French Revolution*. She was never happier. From that point on, we were fellow writers, and for the rest of her life, despite four children and full-time teaching and administrative positions, she matched me book for book.

In 2019, Marilyn was diagnosed with multiple myeloma, a cancer of the plasma cells (antibody-producing white blood cells found in the bone marrow). She was placed on a chemotherapy drug, Revlimid, that precipitated a stroke, leading to an emergency room visit and four days in the hospital. Two weeks after she returned home, we took a brief walk in the park just a block from our home, and Marilyn announced, "I have a book in mind that we should write together. I want to document the difficult days and months before us. Perhaps our trials will be of some use to other couples with one member facing a fatal illness."

Marilyn often suggested topics for books that she or I should undertake, and I replied, "It's a good idea, darling, something you should plunge into. The idea of a joint project is enticing but, as you know, I've already started on a book of stories."

"Oh, no, no—you're not writing *that* book. You're writing *this one* with me! You'll write your chapters and I'll write mine, and they will alternate. It will be *our* book, a book unlike any other book because it entails two minds rather than one, the reflections of a couple who have been married for sixty-five years! A couple very fortunate to have each other as we walk the path that eventually leads to death. You'll walk with your three-wheeled walker, and I'll walk on legs that can ambulate for fifteen or twenty minutes at best."

———

In his 1980 book, *Existential Psychotherapy*, Irv wrote that it is easier to face death if you have few regrets about the life you have lived. In looking back over our long life together, we regret very little. But that doesn't make it any easier to tolerate the bodily travails we now experience day to day, nor does it soften the thought of leaving each other. How can we fight against despair? How do we live meaningfully till the very end?

———

In writing this book, we are at an age when most of our contemporaries have died. We now live each day with the knowledge that our time together is limited and exceedingly precious. We write to make sense of our existence, even as it sweeps us into the darkest zones of physical decline, and death. This book is meant, first and foremost, to help us navigate the end of life.

While this book is obviously an outgrowth of our personal experience, we also see it as part of a national dialogue about end-of-life concerns. Everyone wants to obtain the best medical care available, to find emotional support in family and friends, and to die as painlessly as possible. Even with our medical and social advantages, we are not immune to the pain and fear of oncoming death. Like everyone, we want to preserve the quality of our remaining lives, even as we tolerate medical procedures that sometimes make us sick in the process. How much are we willing to bear to stay alive? How can we end our days as painlessly as possible? How can we gracefully leave this world to the next generation?

We both know that, almost certainly, Marilyn will die of her illness. Together we shall write this journal of what lies ahead in the hope that our experiences and observations will provide meaning and succor not only for us but for our readers.

Irvin D. Yalom   Marilyn Yalom

A
MATTER
OF
DEATH
AND
LIFE

CHAPTER 1
THE VITAL BOX

OVER AND AGAIN I, IRV, FIND myself running my fingers over the upper left part of my chest. For the past month I've had a new object in there, a 2 × 2–inch metal box implanted by a surgeon whose name and face I no longer recall. It all began in a session with a physical therapist whom I had contacted for help with my impaired balance. While taking my pulse at the beginning of our hour, she suddenly turned toward me and, with a shocked look on her face, said, "You and I are going to the ER right now! Your pulse is 30."

I tried to calm her. "It's been slow for months, and I'm asymptomatic."

My words had little impact. She refused to continue our physical therapy session and extracted a promise from me to contact my internist, Dr. W., immediately to discuss the matter.

Three months before, at my annual physical exam, Dr. W. had noted my slow, and occasionally irregular, pulse and referred me to the Stanford arrhythmia clinic. They pasted a

Holter monitor on my chest that recorded my heartbeat for a two-week period. The results showed a consistently slow pulse marked by periodic short bouts of auricular fibrillation. To protect me from throwing off a blood clot to the brain, Dr. W. started me on Eliquis, an anticoagulant. Though Eliquis protected me from a stroke, it promoted a new worry: I had had balance problems for a couple of years, and a serious fall could now be lethal because there is no way to reverse the anticoagulant and halt the bleeding.

When Dr. W. examined me two hours after the physical therapist's referral, he agreed that my pulse had grown even slower and arranged for me to wear a Holter monitor once again to record my heart activity for two weeks.

Two weeks later, after the arrythmia clinic technician removed my Holter monitor and sent the recording of my heart activity to the laboratory for study, another alarming episode occurred, this time to Marilyn: she and I were conversing and, suddenly, she was unable to speak, unable to utter a single word. This persisted for five minutes. Then, over the next several minutes, she slowly regained her ability to speak. Almost certainly, I thought, she had suffered a stroke. Marilyn had been diagnosed with multiple myeloma two months earlier and had begun Revlimid. A stroke could have been caused by this heavy-duty chemotherapy drug she had been taking for the past two weeks. I immediately phoned Marilyn's internist who happened to be nearby and rushed to our home. After a quick examination, she called an ambulance to take Marilyn to the emergency room.

The next few hours in the emergency room waiting area were the worst hours Marilyn and I had ever experienced. The physicians on duty ordered some brain imaging that verified she had indeed had a stroke as a result of a blood clot. They proceeded to administer a drug, TPA (tissue plasminogen activator), to break up the clot. A very small percentage of patients are allergic to this drug—alas, Marilyn was one of those and she almost died in the emergency room. Gradually she recovered with no residua from the stroke and after four days was discharged from the hospital.

But fate was not through with us. Only a few hours after I brought Marilyn home from the hospital, my physician phoned and told me that the results of my heart study had just arrived and that it was essential for me to have an external pacemaker surgically inserted into my thorax. I replied that Marilyn had just arrived home from the hospital and I was entirely preoccupied attending to her. I assured him that I would arrange for admission to surgery early the next week.

"No, no, Irv," my physician replied, "listen to me: this is *not* optional. You *must* get to the emergency room *within the hour* for immediate surgery. Your two-week heart recording showed you had had 3,291 atrial-ventricular blocks lasting a total of one day, six hours."

"Exactly what does that mean?" I asked. My last instruction in cardiac physiology was close to sixty years ago, and I make no pretense of being abreast of medical progress.

"It means," he said, "that in the last two-week period there were over 3,000 occasions when the electrical impulse from your natural pacemaker in the left atrium did not get through to the ventricle below. This resulted in a pause until the ventricle responded erratically to contract the heart on its own. This is life-threatening, and it must be treated immediately."

I immediately checked into the ER where a cardiac surgeon examined me. Three hours later, I was wheeled into the operating room, and an external pacemaker was inserted. Twenty-four hours later I was discharged from the hospital.

———

The bandages have been removed, and the metal box sits in my chest just below the left clavicle. Seventy times a minute this metal gadget commands my heart to contract, and it will continue to do so without any kind of recharge for the next twelve years. It is like no other mechanical device I have ever encountered. Unlike a flashlight that fails to light, a TV remote that will not change channels, a cell phone navigator that will not guide, this tiny device operates with the highest possible stakes: should it fail, my life would end in a matter of minutes. I am stunned by the frailty of my mortality.

So that's my current situation: Marilyn, my dear wife, the most important person in my world since I was 15 years old, is suffering from a grievous illness and my own life feels perilously frail.

And yet, oddly, I am calm, almost serene. Why am I not terrified? Over and again I pose this strange question to myself. For much of my life I've been physically healthy and yet, at some level, always struggled with death anxiety. I believe that my research and writing about death anxiety and my continued attempts to bring relief to patients facing death were fueled by my own personal terror. But, now, what has happened to that terror? Whence cometh my calmness when death veers ever so very much closer?

As days pass, our ordeals fade more into the background. Marilyn and I spend mornings sitting next to one another in our backyard. Admiring the surrounding trees, we hold hands while reminiscing about our life together. We recall our many trips: our two years in Hawaii when I was in the army and we lived on a glorious Kailua beach, our sabbatical year in London, another six months living near Oxford, several months in Paris, other long sojourns in the Seychelles, Bali, France, Austria, and Italy.

After we revel in these exquisite memories, Marilyn squeezes my hand and says, "Irv, there is nothing I would change."

I agree, wholeheartedly.

Both of us feel we've lived our lives fully. Of all the ideas I've employed to comfort patients dreading death, none has been more powerful than the idea of living a regret-free life. Marilyn and I both feel regret-free—we've lived fully and boldly. We were careful not to allow opportunities for exploration to pass us by and now have left little remaining unlived life.

Marilyn goes into the house to nap. Chemotherapy has sapped her energy, and she often sleeps a great deal of the day. I lean back in my chaise lounge and think about the many patients I've seen who were overcome with terror about death—and also of the many philosophers who stared directly at death. Two thousand years ago, Seneca said, "A man cannot stand prepared for death if he has just begun to live. We must make it our aim to have already lived enough." Nietzsche, the most powerful of all phrase makers, said, "Living safely is dangerous." Another phrase of Nietzsche also comes to mind: "Many die too late, and some die too early. Die at the right time!"

Hmm, the right time . . . that hits home. I'm almost 88 and Marilyn 87. Our children and grandchildren are thriving. I fear I've written myself out. I'm in the process of giving up my psychiatric practice, and my wife is now grievously ill.

"Die at the right time." It's hard to push that from consciousness. And then another Nietzschean phrase comes to mind: "What has become perfect, all that is ripe—wants to die. All that is unripe wants to live. All that suffers wants to live, that it may become ripe and joyous and longing—longing for what is further, higher, brighter."

Yes, that, too, comes close to home. Ripeness—that fits. Ripeness is exactly what both Marilyn and I are now experiencing.

———

My thoughts about death stem back to early childhood. I recall that as a youth I was intoxicated by e. e. cummings's poem "Buffalo Bill's Defunct" and recited it to myself many, many times while coasting on my bicycle.

Buffalo Bill's
defunct
     who used to
     ride a watersmooth-silver
         stallion
and break onetwothreefourfive pigeonsjustlikethat
             Jesus
he was a handsome man
        and what i want to know is
how do you like your blue-eyed boy
Mister Death

I was present, or nearly present, at each of my parent's deaths. My father was sitting only a few feet away from me when I saw his head suddenly keel over, his eyes fixed left, looking toward me. I had finished medical school just a month before and grabbed a syringe from my physician brother-in-law's black bag and injected adrenaline into his heart. But it was too late: he was dead from a massive stroke.

Ten years later, my sister and I visited my mother in the hospital: she had fractured her femur. We sat and talked with her for a couple of hours until she was taken into surgery. The two of us took a short walk outside, and when we returned her bed was entirely stripped. Only the bare mattress remained. No more mother.

It's 8:30 on a Saturday morning. My day so far: I woke up about 7 A.M. and, as always, had a small breakfast and walked down the 120-foot path to my office where I opened my computer and checked my email. The first one reads:

My name is M, a student from Iran. I've being treated for panic attacks until my Doctor introduced me to your books and suggested I read *Existential Psychotherapy*. Reading that book, I felt I found the answer to many questions I've faced since my childhood, and I felt you beside me reading each page. Fears, and doubts that nobody but you has answered. I'm reading your books every day, and now it's been several months experiencing no attack. I am so lucky to find you when I had no hope to continue my life. Reading your books make me hopeful. I really don't know how to thank you.

Tears come to my eyes. Letters like this arrive every day—
generally thirty to forty a day—and I feel so blessed to have
the opportunity to help so many. And, because the email is
from Iran, one of our nation's foes, its impact is stronger.
I feel that I join the all-human league of people trying to
help mankind.

I reply to the Iranian student:

I am very happy that my books have been important
and helpful to you. Let us hope that one day our two
countries will regain their senses and compassion for
one another.

My very best wishes to you—Irv Yalom

I am always touched by my fan letters, though, at times,
I am overwhelmed with their number. I make an attempt
to answer each letter, taking care to mention each writer by
name so they know I've read their letter. I store them in an
email file marked "fans" which I started a few years ago and
which now has several thousand entries. I mark this letter
with a star—I plan to reread the starred letters some day in
the future when my spirits are very low and need bolstering.

It is now 10 A.M., and I step out of my office. Just outside I have a view of our bedroom window and glance up at
the house. I see that Marilyn is awake and has opened the
curtains. She is still very weak from her chemotherapy injection three days ago, and I rush back to the house to prepare
her some breakfast. But she's already had some apple juice
and has appetite for nothing else. She lies on the living room
couch taking in the view of the oak trees in our garden.

As always, I ask how she is feeling.

As always, she answers candidly, "I feel awful. I can't put it into words. I am removed from everything . . . terrible feelings run through my body. If it weren't for you, I wouldn't stay alive . . . I don't want to live anymore . . . I'm so sorry to keep saying this to you. I know I'm saying it over and over."

I've been hearing her speak this way every day for several weeks. I feel despondent and helpless. Nothing brings me more pain than her pain: each week she has a chemotherapy infusion that leaves her nauseated, headachy, and greatly fatigued. She feels out of touch with her body, and with everything and everyone in ineffable ways. Many patients treated with chemotherapy refer to this as "chemo brain." I encourage her to walk even 100 feet to the mailbox but, as usual, I am unsuccessful. I hold her hand and try every way I know to reassure her.

Today, when she again states her unwillingness to continue living like this, I answer in a different fashion. "Marilyn, we've spoken several times about the California law giving physicians the right to assist patients to end their life if they are suffering greatly from an untreatable fatal disease. Remember how our friend, Alexandra, did exactly that? So many times over the last couple of months you have said you're staying alive only for me and worrying about how I'll survive without you. I've been thinking about that a lot. Last night in bed I lay awake for hours thinking about it. I want you to hear this. Listen to me: *I will survive your death.* I can continue to live—probably not too long, considering the little metal box in my chest. I can't deny that I will miss you every day of my life . . . but I can continue to live. I'm no longer terrorized by death . . . not like before.

"Remember how I felt after my knee surgery when I had a stroke that permanently cost me my balance and forced me to walk with a cane or walker? Remember how miserable and depressed I was? Enough to send me back into therapy. Well, you know that has passed. I'm more tranquil now—I'm no longer tormented—I'm even sleeping pretty well.

"What I want you to know is this: I can survive your death. What I cannot bear is the thought of you living with such pain, such agony for my sake."

Marilyn looks deeply into my eyes. This time my words have touched her. We sit together, holding hands, for a very long time. One of Nietzsche's sentences passes through my mind: "*The thought of suicide is a great consolation: by means of it one gets through many a dark night.*" But I keep that to myself.

Marilyn closes her eyes for a while, then nods, "Thank you for saying that. You've never said this before. It's a relief . . . I know these months have been a nightmare for you. You've had to do everything—shopping, cooking, taking me to the doctor's and to the clinic and waiting for me for hours, dressing me, calling all my friends. I know I've exhausted you. But, yet, right now you seem to be feeling all right. You seem so balanced, so steady. You've told me several times that if you could, you would take my disease for me. And I know you would. You've always taken care of me, always lovingly, but lately you're different."

"How?"

"Hard to describe. Sometimes you seem at peace. Almost tranquil. Why is that? How have you done it?"

"That's the big question. I don't know myself. But I have a hunch and it's not related to my love for you. You know I've loved you since we met as teenagers. It's about something else."

"Tell me." Marilyn now sits up and looks at me intently.

"I think it's this." I pat the metal box in my chest.

"You mean, your heart? But why tranquility?"

"This box I am always touching and rubbing keeps reminding me that I'll die of my heart trouble, probably suddenly and quickly. I won't die like John died or all the others we saw on his dementia ward."

Marilyn nods; she understands. John was a close friend with severe dementia who had died recently in a nearby residence for the aged. The last time I visited him he did not recognize me or anyone else: he just stood there and screamed and screamed for hours. I cannot erase this image from my memory: it's my nightmare of a death.

"Now, thanks to what's going on in my chest," I say, touching my metal box, "I believe I'll die swiftly—like my father."

CHAPTER 2

BECOMING AN INVALID

EVERY DAY I, MARILYN, LIE on the sofa in our living room and look out through the floor-to-ceiling windows at the oaks and evergreens that live on our property. It is now springtime, and I have watched green leaves reappear on our magnificent valley oak. Earlier today I saw an owl perch on the spruce between the front of our house and Irv's office. I can see a bit of the vegetable garden that our son Reid planted with tomatoes, green beans, cucumbers, and squash. He wants me to think about vegetables ripening in the summer, when I will presumably "be better."

For the last few months, since I was diagnosed with multiple myeloma, placed on heavy medication, and hospitalized after a stroke, I have been mostly miserable. My weekly chemotherapy injections are followed relentlessly by days of nausea and other forms of bodily suffering, the description of which I shall spare my readers. I am exhausted most of the time—as if cotton is stuffed around my brain or a foggy veil exists between me and the rest of the world.

I've had several friends who have had breast cancer, and only now do I have some understanding of what they went through to combat their disease. Chemotherapy, radiation, surgery, support groups have all been part of their everyday lives as breast cancer patients. Twenty-five years ago, when I wrote *A History of the Breast*, breast cancer was still thought of as a "terminal" illness. Today doctors refer to it as a "chronic" disease that can be treated and arrested. I envy breast cancer patients because when they go into remission, they can stop chemotherapy. Multiple myeloma patients generally require continuation of treatment, though less frequently than the once-a-week injections I now endure. Again and again, I keep asking myself: *Is it worth it?*

I am 87 years old. Eighty-seven is a ripe time to die. When I look at the obituary columns in the *San Francisco Chronicle* and the *New York Times*, I note that most of the deaths occur to people in their eighties or younger. The average age of death in the United States is 79 years. Even in Japan, which has the best national record for longevity, the average age is 87.32 for women. After the very satisfying long life I have shared with Irv and the good health I have enjoyed for most of my life, why should I want to live now with daily misery and despair?

The simple answer is that there is no easy way to die. If I refuse the treatment, I shall die painfully of multiple myeloma sooner rather than later. In California, physician aid in dying is legal. I could, when I am nearing the end, request assisted suicide from a physician.

But there is another, more complicated answer to the question of whether I should stay alive. Throughout this excruciating period, I have become more aware of the extent to which my life is connected with the lives of others—not only with my husband and children, but also with the many friends who continue to support me in my time of need. These friends have written multiple messages of encouragement, they have brought food to the house and sent flowers and plants. An old friend from college sent me a soft, cuddly bathrobe, and another knitted me a woolen shawl. Over and over again I realize how blessed I am to have such friends, in addition to my family members. Ultimately, I have come to the understanding that one stays alive not only for oneself, but also for others. Though this insight may be self-evident, only now do I realize it fully.

Because of my Stanford affiliation with the Institute for Research on Women (which I officially administered between 1976 and 1987), I established a network of women scholars and supporters, many of whom have become my close friends. For fifteen years, from 2004 to 2019, I ran a literary salon at my home in Palo Alto and apartment in San Francisco for Bay Area women writers, which added considerably to my friendship circle. Moreover, as a former professor of French, I spent time in France and other European countries whenever I could. Yes, I've had an enviable position that provided the opportunities to establish such friendships. I am comforted by the thought that my life or death matters to friends around the world—in France, Cambridge, New York, Dallas, Hawaii, Greece, Switzerland, and in California.

Fortunately for us, our four children—Eve, Reid, Victor, and Ben—all live in California, three of them in the Bay Area and the fourth in San Diego. In these past few months, they have been very present in our lives, spending days and nights at the house, cooking meals, and lifting our spirits. Eve, a physician, has brought me medical marijuana gummies, and

I take a half of one before dinner to counter the nausea and give me appetite. They seem to work better than any of the other meds and have no noticeable side effects.

Lenore, our granddaughter from Japan, has been living with us this year while working at a Silicon Valley biotech startup. At first, I was able to help her adjust to American life—now it is she who has been taking care of me. She helps us with computer and television issues, and adds Japanese cooking to our diet. We shall greatly miss her when she goes off to graduate school at Northwestern University in a few months.

But, most of all, it is Irv who sustains me. He has been the most loving of caretakers—patient, understanding, committed to lessening my misery. I've not driven our car for five months, and aside from the time our children visit, Irv does all the shopping for food and all the cooking. He drives me to and from medical appointments, and stays with me during my several-hour infusions. He figures out the television possibilities in the evening and sits through programs even when they are far from his first choice. I'm not writing this praise to flatter him or make him seem like a saint to my readers. This is the unadorned truth as I have experienced it.

Often I contrast my situation with that of patients who have no loving partner or friend and who are obliged to undergo treatment on their own. As I sat recently in the Stanford Infusion Center, waiting for my chemo injection, the woman next to me said she was alone in life but found support in her Christian faith. Even though she has to negotiate her medical visits without someone at her side, she feels the presence of God near her at all times. Though I am not a believer myself, I was glad for her. And similarly, I have been heartened by the friends who tell me they are praying for me. My Bahai friend, Vida, prays for me every day, and if there is a God, her fervent prayers must have been heard. Other friends—Catholic, Protestant, Jewish, and Muslim—have also written to say I am in their prayers. The writer Gail Sheehy moved me to tears when she wrote: "I will pray for you and I will imagine you being cupped in God's hand. You are just tiny enough to fit."

Irv and I, culturally Jewish, do not believe that we shall be conscious after death. And yet, the words of the Hebrew Bible sustain me: "Yeah, though I walk through the valley of the shadow of death, I will fear no evil" (Psalm 23). These words circulate in my mind, among others from religious and nonreligious sources that I committed to memory long ago.

"Oh death, where is thy sting?" (1 Corinthians)

"The worst is death, and death will have his day." (Shakespeare, *Richard II*)

And there is "The Bustle in a House," a lovely verse by Emily Dickinson:

The sweeping up the Heart
And putting love away
We shall not want to use again
Until Eternity—

All of these familiar poetic phrases take on new meaning in my present situation, as I lie on the sofa and reflect. Certainly I cannot follow the advice of Dylan Thomas: "Rage, rage against the dying of the light." There is not enough life force left in me for that. I feel more in touch with some of the prosaic inscriptions that my son Reid and I found when we photographed cemetery tombstones for our 2008 book, *The American Resting Place*. One is fresh in my mind: "To live in hearts we leave behind is not to die." To live in the hearts we leave behind—or, as Irv so often puts it, to "ripple" into the lives of those who have known us personally or through our writing, or to follow the counsel of Saint Paul when he wrote: "though I have faith, so that I could remove mountains, and have not charity, I am nothing" (1 Corinthians 13).

Paul's take on the primacy of charity is always worth re-reading, for it reminds us that love, meaning kindness to others and compassion for their suffering, trumps all the other virtues. (The feminist in me is always taken aback when I read what follows in Corinthians: that women should "keep silence in the churches, for it is not permitted unto them to speak" and that "if they will learn anything, let them ask their husbands at home; for it is a shame for women to speak in the church." When I read this, I chuckle to myself remembering Reverend Jane Shaw's many magnificent sermons in the Stanford Chapel.)

Henry James has revised Paul's words on charity into a clever formula:

> Three things in human life are important. The first is to be kind. The second is to be kind. And the third is to be kind.

I hope to adhere to this dictum even as I anguish over my personal situation.

———

I know many women who bravely faced their deaths or the death of their spouses. In February 1954, when I returned from Wellesley College to Washington, DC, for my father's funeral, my grieving mother's first words to me were "You have to be very brave." Always a model of kindness, her concern for her daughters was paramount as she buried her husband of twenty-seven years. Dad was only 54 and had died suddenly of a heart attack while deep-sea fishing in Florida.

Several years later, my mother married again. And she ultimately ended up marrying and burying four husbands! She lived to know her grandchildren and even some of her great-grandchildren. After a move to California to be nearer to us, she died peacefully at the age of 92 ½. I always assumed that I would die at her age—but now I know I will not make it into the nineties.

A close friend, Susan Bell, almost reached ninety. Susan had escaped death more than once in her life: she had fled the Nazi invasion of Czechoslovakia in 1939 accompanying her mother to London and leaving behind a father who died in the Terezin Concentration Camp. She and her parents had all been baptized as Lutherans, but the Nazis looked to Susan's four Jewish grandparents as reason to threaten her life and kill her father.

A few weeks before she died Susan gave me a precious gift—her nineteenth-century English silver teapot. Tea from that pot had kept us alert years earlier as she and I worked on our 1990 book, *Revealing Lives*, an edited collection of articles on autobiography, biography, and gender. Susan had been a pioneer in developing the field of women's history and continued that work as an affiliated scholar at the Stanford Clayman Institute until the end of her life. She died suddenly in July 2015, in the swimming pool at the age of 89 ½.

But perhaps more that anyone, it is Diane Middlebrook who is my role model of how I would like to behave in

the months to come. Stanford professor of English and ac-
claimed biographer of poets Anne Sexton, Sylvia Plath, and
Ted Hughes, Diane became a close friend for over twenty-five
years until her untimely death from cancer in 2007. When I
saw her in the hospital shortly before her death, she received
Irv and me with grace, communicated her love for us, and
kissed us each good-bye. I noticed how respectfully she ad-
dressed the nurses as they came in and out of the room.
Diane was only 68 years old when she left us.

There is one more person whose decline and death has
greatly affected me: the noted French scholar René Girard.
René had been my dissertation director in the late fifties
and early sixties at Johns Hopkins, but I really didn't get to
know him as a close colleague and friend until he came to
Stanford decades later. Then, with his wife Martha, I felt a
new connection that lasted until his death in 2015.

That connection was oddly the strongest during his last
years when he was unable to speak due to a series of strokes.
Instead of talking, I would sit next to him, hold his hand,
and look into his eyes. He always seemed to enjoy the jars of
homemade apricot jam I brought to him.

The last time we were together, he saw a jack rabbit
running outside past the window and exclaimed in French:
"Un lapin!" Somehow those words emerged in spite of the
brain damage that had blocked all speech. When I had a
stroke and for a few minutes lost the ability to speak, I immediately thought of René. It was such an odd experience
to have thoughts in your brain that you simply cannot turn
into speech.

I am so grateful I quickly recovered my speech without
obvious residual effects. I can't remember a time when I

did not enjoy talking. When I was four or five, my mother took me to elocution lessons, where we curtsied to Miss Betty and recited poems for an audience of other children and their proud mothers. Since then, throughout my life I have taken pleasure in public speaking, in addition to private conversations.

But today, I am exhausted by lengthy conversation. I limit myself to a half an hour with friends who drop by. Even an extended phone call tires me out.

When I despair of my condition, I try to remember all the reasons why I should still be grateful. I can still talk, read, and answer my emails. I am surrounded by loving people in a comfortable and attractive home. There is hope that the chemotherapy treatments will be reduced in dosage and frequency, and that I shall be able to live a semi-normal life again, though right now I don't believe that shall ever be the case. I am trying to resign myself to the life of an invalid, or at least the life of a convalescent, as one referred politely to people like me in the past.

CHAPTER 3

AWARENESS OF EVANESCENCE

THREE VERY CLOSE FRIENDS, Herb Kotz, Larry Zaroff, and Oscar Dodek, died over the last few years. I knew them in high school and college, and they had been my cadaver-mates in anatomy class during our first year of medical school. We had remained close all our lives. Now all three are gone, and I have become the holder of memories of our time together. Though the events of our first year of medical school took place over sixty years ago, they are still vivid and palpable. Indeed, I have the strange notion that, if one opened the correct door and peered in, miraculously there we'd be, the four of us in the flesh, for all to see, all busily dissecting tendons and arteries, joking with one another, and my friend Larry, who had already decided to become a surgeon, peering at my untidy dissection and pronouncing that my decision to become a psychiatrist was a truly blessed moment for the world of surgery.

One particular memory of our anatomy course is deeply etched in my mind. It involves a horrible incident that occurred on the day we were to begin the removal and dissection of the brain. When lifting the black plastic cover from our cadaver we spotted a large roach sitting in one of the eye sockets. We were all grossed out—I more than the others, for I had grown up terrified of the roaches that often scuttled across the floor of my father's grocery store and our apartment above the store.

After quickly replacing the black tarpaulin, I persuaded the others to take a pass on dissection that day and, instead, play a couple of rubbers of bridge. The four of us had often played bridge at lunch, and for the next couple of weeks, our group of four played bridge instead of attending anatomy lab. Though I became a better bridge player, I am ashamed to admit that I, who have spent my life studying the human mind, skipped the dissection of the brain!

But what is truly unsettling is the knowledge that these vivid, tangible, emotion-laden events exist only in my own mind. Yes, yes, of course that is obvious—everyone knows that. Yet, deep down I somehow never really owned it, never grasped that no one but me can open the door to the space containing these scenes. There *is* no door, no room, no ongoing dissection. My past world exists only in the buzzing neurons of my brain. When I, the only one of the four still alive, die—poof—all will evaporate and these memories will vanish forever. When I truly hold this, acknowledge and own this, then the ground under my feet no longer feels firm.

But, wait! As I examine once again my memory of our bridge game in the back of the empty lecture hall, I suddenly realize there's something wrong. Remember this took place over sixty-five years ago! Anyone who has tried to write a memoir learns that memory is a fickle, elusive entity. I realize that one of our four bridge players, Larry Zaroff, was such a dedicated student and so committed to becoming a surgeon that there was no way in the world he would skip an anatomy dissection class to play bridge. I shut my eyes forcefully and squint more closely at my memory and suddenly realize that the bridge game consisted of Herb, Oscar, me, and Larry—but not Larry Zaroff. It was another Larry, a student named Larry Eanet. And then I remember that our dissecting team consisted of *six* students: for some reason there had been an acute shortage of cadavers that year and six students, rather than four, were assigned to dissect a cadaver.

I remember my friend, Larry Eanet, well: he was a wonderfully talented pianist who played at all our junior high and high school events and dreamed of becoming a professional musician. His parents, however, immigrants like mine, pressured him to go to medical school. Larry was a lovely man, and though I was tone deaf, he always strove to arouse my musical sensibilities. Shortly before we began medical school, he took me to a record store and selected six great classical recordings for me to buy. Over and again I listened to these records while studying but, alas, by the end of the first year, I am embarrassed to say that I had great difficulty discriminating one from the other.

Larry chose to go into dermatology because he believed that was the specialty that would give him the most freedom to pursue his musical career. Later he played piano for such visiting musicians as Dizzy Gillespie, Stan Getz, and Cab Calloway. How wonderful it would be to reminisce with Larry! I decide to contact him, but when I look him up on Google, I learn that, alas, he, too, had died, ten years before. Oh, how he would have smiled to read the heading of his *Washington Post* obituary: "Jazz Pianist Virtuoso Moonlighted as a Doctor"!

The sixth student of our team was Elton Herman, whom I knew from our undergraduate days together—an intelligent, sweet, most agreeable student, a lumbering lad prone to wearing corduroy knickers to class. How was Elton? Where was he? I always liked him and wanted to hear his voice again. But when I search online, I learn that he, too, is dead. Eight years dead. All five of my mates dead! My head begins to swim. I close my eyes, concentrate on the past, and, for a moment, I see us all together, arms around one another's shoulder. We six were so strong, so hopeful for the future, so eager to succeed, six smart and accomplished students starting medical school together. All of us so dedicated to learning and so full of dreams of success and, yet, five of us, everyone but me, dead and buried. Nothing but desiccated bones by now. Of the six of us, I alone still walk the earth. I tremble as I think of this. Why had I outlasted them? Sheer luck. I feel blessed to still breathe and think and smell and to hold hands with my wife. But I'm lonely. I miss them. My time is coming.

———

This story has an afterlife. On two occasions, I have told it to patients with excellent effects. One was a woman who, within the previous two months, had lost her husband and father—the two people closest and dearest to her. She said that she had already consulted with two therapists, but both seemed so distant and uninvolved that she could make no connection with either. I began to imagine that she would soon feel similarly about me. Indeed, throughout our consultation she seemed frozen, blunted, difficult to reach. I felt a yawning gulf between us and obviously she shared that feeling: toward the end of our hour she commented, "For weeks I've felt that everything is unreal and that I'm entirely alone. I feel as though I'm riding in a train somewhere and the seats are all empty: there are no other passengers."

"I knew exactly what you feel," I responded. "I've recently had a similar experience." I then proceeded to tell her the story about my five medical school classmates whom I had lost and how my sense of reality had been shaken.

She listened intently, leaning toward me, tears streaming down her face, and said, "Yes, yes, I understand. I understand perfectly: it's *exactly* what I'm experiencing. My tears are celebrating: there *is* someone else on the train after all. You know what I've just been thinking? That we should both bless life and bask in the realness right now, now while it's still real."

Those words staggered me, and we sat in convivial silence for a long time.

A couple of weeks later I told the story again. I had my final meeting with a patient I had been seeing weekly for the past year. She lived a thousand miles away, and we had been meeting on the computer via Zoom. For our final meeting, however, she chose to fly to California to meet me face-to-face for the first time.

We had had a tempestuous course of therapy, and I had never fully satisfied her desire for paternal love and understanding. I tried hard, but no matter how much I offered, she was often dissatisfied and critical of me. I had been seeing patients via video for years and had come to believe that my Zoom therapy and my face-to-face therapy were equally effective, but my work with this patient raised some doubts in my mind. These were tempered when I learned that she was similarly dissatisfied with two previous therapists whom she had met face to face for considerably longer periods of time.

As I waited for her to arrive, I wondered how it would feel to see the patient in person. Would it be the same, or would I be jolted by the difference, the strangeness, of seeing her in the flesh? We shook hands when we started the hour, holding on to each other slightly longer than an ordinary handshake. It was as though we had to reassure ourselves of the other person's materiality.

I proceeded to do what I generally do in a final session. I had reviewed my notes, and I set about describing my recollections of our first meetings. I reviewed some of her reasons for contacting me and tried to open a discussion of what we had done and how we had worked together.

She had little interest in my words. Her attention was elsewhere. "Dr. Yalom, I've been thinking . . . we started with a contract for a year's therapy of weekly meetings and by my count we've met forty-six times not fifty-two times. I know that I was on a month's vacation and you were also away but, even so, it seems to me that you owe me six more sessions."

I was in no way put off by this. We had discussed this issue on other occasions, and I reminded her that I had mentioned our ending date more than once. I replied, "I'm taking your comment to mean that our work has been important to you and you want us to continue. As I've said to you before, I have so much respect for how hard you've worked and how tenacious and dedicated to our work you've been, even at times when you've been in a lot of pain. So, I'm going to take your request for those six more sessions as an expression of how much I have meant to you. Am I right?"

"Yes, you've meant a lot to me and, yes, you know how hard it is for me to say this. And, yes, it's very hard to let you go. I know I'm going to have to be satisfied with the image of you stored in my brain. And I know only too well that it's an image that will slowly fade away. Nothing is permanent, everything is insubstantial."

We were silent for a few moments and then I repeated her words, "everything is insubstantial." I continued, "Your words bring to mind something I too have been experiencing. Let me tell you about it." Then I proceeded to recount the entire story of the death of my five classmates and how I had also been struggling with the same concept—*that everything is insubstantial.*

After I had finished, we sat in silence for a long time, past the end of our hour. Then, she said, "Thank you, Irv, for sharing that story. It felt like a great gift. A tremendous gift." As we stood to end our session, she said, "I'd like a hug—one that I can carry with me for a long time. A substantial hug."

CHAPTER 4

WHY DON'T WE MOVE TO ASSISTED LIVING?

SEVERAL YEARS AGO, Irv and I investigated the option of moving to an assisted living facility. The one popular with Stanford people, if they can afford it, is Vi, located only a few blocks away from Stanford University. There are two other nearby assisted living facilities, Channing House in downtown Palo Alto and The Sequoias, in a lovely rustic setting a bit farther away. All three provide meals and have different levels of service, ranging from assistance with everyday tasks to hospice care. We enjoyed going to dinner at Vi and the Sequoias with friends who reside there, and we could see that such a residential center had many attractions. But because we had no grave health issues at the time, we held back from making a commitment.

Our colleague, Eleanor Maccoby, the first woman professor of psychology at Stanford, died at Vi at the age of 101. For more than a dozen years, she ran their weekly current affairs discussion, and in her very last years, she wrote a remarkable autobiography. We went to the well-attended funeral service in her honor and were happy to see other friends still alive and doing well.

Sometimes we ask ourselves: Are we making a mistake by not going to assisted living? Certainly it would be convenient to have the round-the-clock care. And having meals prepared and served to you is always a blessing. But the thought of leaving our home of forty-plus years with its verdant garden and trees deters us. We are simply not willing to give up this house and setting, not to mention the separate office where Irv writes and still sees an occasional patient.

Fortunately, we are in a financial position that allows us to keep our house and to make some necessary changes. When it became apparent that I would have difficulty negotiating the stairs to the second floor where our bedroom is located, we put in an electric stair chair. Now I ride up and down like a princess in a private coach.

Perhaps, more than anything, we are able to stay in this house because we have the continued services of our housekeeper, Gloria, who has been with us for over twenty-five years. Gloria takes care of us, as well as the house. She finds our lost glasses and cell phones. She cleans up after our meals, changes the bed linens, and waters the plants. How many people in America are lucky enough to have someone like Gloria in their lives? Our "luck" depends obviously on our financial situation, but even so, it is more than that. Gloria is exceptional. She has raised three sons and a granddaughter while working for us and negotiating difficult mid-life problems, including a divorce. We do everything we can do to make her life comfortable, including—of course—paying a good wage, social security, and an annual paid vacation.

Yes, we know, few people can afford to have a housekeeper, just as few Americans can afford assisted living.

Assisted living, depending on location and services, now costs many thousands of dollars per month. Adam Gopnik in the *New Yorker* (May 20, 2019) states that less than 10 percent of the elderly go into nursing homes or assisted living because most prefer to stay in their homes; and even if they wanted to, many do not have the means.

We, too, have opted to stay in our home, but for emotional rather than practical reasons. We built this house over a period of ten years, haphazardly adding new areas and ultimately creating a livable, lovable space. How many birthday parties, book parties, weddings, and wedding receptions have we celebrated in the living room or outside on the back patio or on the front lawn? From our second-story bedroom window, we can see birds nesting in the branches of our towering oak tree. And the other upstairs bedrooms, now devoid of teenagers, are available for visiting children, grandchildren, and friends. We also invite out-of-town guests to stay with us whenever they are in the Bay Area.

And then there are the possessions—furniture, books, art objects, and souvenirs scattered throughout the house. How could we crowd all of these into a much smaller living space? Though we have started giving away some items to our children, it would be painful to live without most of them, for each has a story that recalls a specific time of our lives and often a memorable incident.

The two wooden Japanese dogs in the hallway were purchased on Portobello Road in London in 1968. We were leaving England after a year's sabbatical and had exactly thirty-two pounds in our British bank account. When we saw the dogs—the male baring his teeth, the female with her mouth closed (!)—I suspected they were old and precious. I asked the shopkeeper what he knew about them, and all he could tell us was that he had brought them from someone who had just returned from Asia. We offered him the thirty-two pounds that were still in the bank, and he accepted. They were shipped home along with a few other purchases and have been a treasured part of our interior landscape ever since.

A carved Egyptian head that once plugged an ancient canopic jar containing a dead person's organs (stomach, intestines, lungs, or liver) sits atop a shelf in the living room. We purchased it from a Parisian antique dealer some thirty-five years ago. The accompanying certificate states that it represents Amset, one of the four sons of Horus, who was the Egyptian national protective deity. I have loved looking into the fish-shaped eyes outlined in black of this solemn figure. Although Irv and I never traveled together to Egypt, Eve, our daughter, and I had that pleasure several years ago with a Wellesley travel group. Visiting museums and mosques in Cairo, traveling by boat up the Nile, and seeing the pyramids and temples left me keenly interested in ancient Egypt.

Throughout the house there are visual reminders of our two months' sabbatical stay in Bali—masks, paintings, and fabrics that evoke a place where aesthetics are a way of life. The large carved mask that hangs over our fireplace has bulging eyes, golden ear flaps, and a thin red tongue that sticks out between two rows of menacing teeth. Another Balinese object, the small wood carving over the door at the foot of the stairs, is more playful: it shows a winged dragon with its tail in its mouth. Upstairs there are cloth paintings of Balinese landscapes with stylized birds and foliage. In Bali you often see the same scene depicted over and over again, because there is no sense that a work of art has to be "original." All artists have a right to the same material, which constitutes a kind of visual mythology.

Who will want all these objects? Just because they appeal to us and hold our memories does not mean that our children will desire them. When we die the stories attached to each one of our possessions will ultimately disappear. Well, maybe not entirely. We still possess items inherited from our parents that are referred to as "grandma's table" or "Uncle Morton's Wedgwood." Our children have grown up with these items and remember their original owners, Irv's mother, Rivka, who furnished her DC house with fashionable items from the fifties, and Uncle Morton, Irv's sister's husband, an ardent collector of antique Wedgwood, paperweights, and coins. "Grandma's" card table, a neo-baroque red, black, and gold anomaly that is housed in our sunroom, has been the setting of numerous chess and pinochle games which Irv played with his father and now plays with his sons. Any of our three sons will be glad to have it.

Recently our son Ben's wife, Anisa, commented on some embroidered fabrics that we had framed and hung in different rooms. I told her that we had found them in an open market in China when we were there in 1987 and you could buy such treasures very cheaply. Anisa and Ben have a particular interest in fabrics, so I said they could have the Chinese embroideries. "Just remember to tell your children that Nana and Zeyda bought them in China long, long ago."

But our greatest problem will be disposing of our books, some three to four thousand of them. They are arranged, more or less, in categories—psychiatric texts, women's studies, French and German, novels, poetry, philosophy, classics, art, cookbooks, and foreign translations of both of our publications. Look into any room (except the dining room) and into several of the closets, and you will find books, books, books. We have been book people all our lives, and even though Irv now reads largely on an iPad, we still seem to be acquiring books in their familiar paper form. Every few months we send boxes of books to the local public library or to other nonprofit organizations, but that scarcely makes a dent in the wall-to-wall shelves that line most of our rooms.

There is a special section for books that were written by friends, several of whom are no longer with us. They recall our friendship with the British poet, novelist, and nonfiction writer Alex Comfort, best known for *The Joy of Sex*. After suffering a stroke, he was bound to a wheelchair and had great trouble moving his arms and legs, so we are particularly moved by the short, wiggly dedication he wrote to us in a book of poems. We also have a number of books by Ted Roszak, my colleague at Cal State Hayward. We remember him as a highly original historian and novelist, whose 1969 book *The Making of a Counterculture* added a new term to the English vocabulary. Ted's analysis of the "counterculture" brings to mind anti–Vietnam War protests, the Berkeley free speech movement, and all the political upheavals we lived through in the 1960s. And there are the books by Stanford professors Albert Guerard, Joseph Frank, and John Felstiner—all friends who graced our lives for many years and left behind major works of literary criticism. Albert was a specialist in the English novel, Joe was the foremost Dostoevsky scholar of his age, and John was the translator of Pablo Neruda and Paul Celan. What do we do with such treasured works?

One collection of books stands apart under glass doors: our Dickens collection. Irv started collecting Dickens's first editions and parts when we were in London in 1967 and 1968. Most of Dickens's works were published in monthly parts that were then bound up into book form. Over the years, whenever Irv saw a Dickens book listed in one of several catalogs that came to us from various British dealers, he would check to see if we already owned it, and if not, he would order it—that is, depending on the price. We still don't have a good copy of *A Christmas Carol* because it has always had too hefty a price tag.

Our youngest son, Ben, would open the packages with Irv and look at the engravings even before he could read. At the sight of the newest arrival he would exclaim, "It smells like Dickens." All of our children have read some of Dickens, but Ben, a theater director, has probably read the most. It is understood that the Dickens collection will go to him.

As for the rest of the books, it's difficult even to give them away. Will our photographer son, Reid, want all the art books? Will our psychologist son, Victor, want Irv's therapy books? Will anyone want my German books or those in women's studies? Fortunately, a good friend, Marie-Pierre Ulloa in the Stanford French Department has offered to take my large collection of books in French. A few dealers will come to the house and pick through our holdings which have resale value, but otherwise our precious books will probably be scattered to the winds.

For now, they are still housed in our home and Irv's office. It is comforting to move among familiar objects for the last period of our life. We are grateful that we can stay in our house and will move to assisted living or a nursing home only as a last resort.

CHAPTER 5

RETIREMENT: THE PRECISE MOMENT OF DECISION

I'VE BEEN GINGERLY APPROACHING retirement for several years, testing it out in small doses. Psychotherapy has been my life's work and the thought of giving it up is painful. I took my first step toward retirement when, a few years ago, I decided to inform all my new patients in our first session that I would see them for only one year.

There are many reasons why I hate to retire from being a therapist. Mainly it's because I so enjoy being helpful to others—and by this time of life I've gotten good at it. Another reason, and I say this with some embarrassment, is that I will miss listening to so many stories. I have an insatiable thirst for stories, especially those that I can use in my teaching and writing. I've been in love with stories since I was a child and, aside from my medical school years, have always, without fail, read myself to sleep. Though I am transfixed by the great stylists such as Joyce, Nabokov, and Banville, it is the consummate storytellers—Dickens, Trollope, Hardy,

Chekhov, Murakami, Dostoevsky, Auster, McEwan—whom I truly adore.

Allow me to tell you a story about the precise moment I learned it was time to retire from being a therapist.

On July 4th, a couple of weeks ago, I returned home a few minutes before 4 P.M. from a holiday fete in a nearby neighborhood park and entered my office intending to spend an hour responding to emails. No sooner had I sat down at my desk than I heard a knock on my door. I opened it to find an attractive, middle-aged woman standing there.

"Hello," I greeted her. "I'm Irv Yalom. Were you looking for me?"

"I'm Emily. I'm a psychotherapist from Scotland, and I have an appointment with you today at 4 P.M."

My heart sank. Oh, no, once again my memory had failed me!

"Please come in," I said, trying to be nonchalant, "let me check my schedule." I opened my appointment book and was shocked to see "Emily A." writ large at my 4 P.M. slot. I never thought to check my schedule this morning. Never, in my right mind, that is, if I were in my right mind, would I schedule someone on the Fourth of July. The rest of my family was still at the holiday celebration at the nearby park, and it was by sheer chance that I had returned early and was in my office when she appeared.

"I'm so sorry, Emily, but, this being a national holiday, I didn't even check my schedule. You've come a long way to be here?"

"Quite far. But my husband had professional reasons to come to Los Angeles so I would have been in this part of the world anyway."

That offered some relief: at least she hadn't made the long trip from Scotland specifically for a session with someone who hadn't bothered to remember her. I tried to make her comfortable: I pointed to a chair. "Please sit, Emily, I can make myself free and meet with you now. But please excuse me for a few minutes. I must notify my family that I'm not to be interrupted."

I hurried back to my home only a hundred feet or so away and left a note for Marilyn about my unexpected appointment, grabbed my hearing aids (I don't often use them, but Emily had a soft voice), and returned to my office. As I sat down at my desk, I opened my computer.

"Emily, I'm almost ready to begin, but first I'll need a couple minutes to reread your email message to me." While I scanned my computer trying, in vain, to locate Emily's email, she began weeping loudly. I turned to face her, and she held out to me a folded sheet of paper retrieved from her purse.

"Here's the email you're looking for. I brought it along because the last time we met, five years ago, you also couldn't find my email." She continued to weep even more loudly.

I read the first sentence in her email: "We met together on two earlier occasions over the last ten years (for a total of four sessions) and you have helped me a great deal and . . ." I could read no farther: Emily now began to wail loudly, saying over and again, "I'm invisible, I'm invisible. Four times we've met and you don't know me."

In shock, I put her note away and turned to her. Tears streamed down her face. In vain, she searched her purse for a Kleenex and then reached toward my box of Kleenex on the table next to her chair but, alas, it was empty, and I had to go into the lavatory to bring her the few sheets of toilet paper that were left on the spool. I prayed hard she would not need more.

As we sat silently for a short time, reality broke through! This was the moment when I realized, truly realized, I was obviously not fit to continue my practice. My memory was too impaired. So I doffed my professional bearing, closed my computer and turned to her. "I'm so very sorry, Emily. What a nightmare this meeting has been so far."

We sat in silence for a few moments as she recovered her composure and I understood what I had to do. "Emily, I want to say a few things to you. First, you've traveled a long way here with hopes and expectations about our session, and I'm very willing to spend the next hour with you and offer all that I can. But, because I've already caused you such distress, there is no way I can possibly accept any fee for our session today. Second, I want to address your feeling of being invisible. Please listen to me and hear what I must say: *my forgetting you has nothing to do with you and everything to do with me*. Let me tell you some things about my life right now."

Emily stopped weeping, wiped her eyes with a handkerchief, and leaned forward in her chair, highly attentive.

"First, I must tell you that my wife of sixty-five years is now quite ill with cancer and undergoing some extremely unpleasant chemotherapy. I'm extremely shaken by this, and my ability to focus on my work is impaired. Also I want to tell you that, recently, I've been questioning whether my memory was too impaired to continue practicing as a therapist."

As I spoke, I was highly suspicious of myself: I was, in effect, saying it's the stress of bearing up under my wife's illness—it's not me. I felt ashamed of myself: I know that my memory was ailing before my wife got sick. I remember

RETIREMENT 39

taking a walk with another colleague several months before
and sharing my concerns about my memory. I described my
morning toilet and how after I had finished shaving, I had
forgotten entirely whether I had already brushed my teeth.
It was only when I discovered the brush was wet that I knew
I had already used it. I remember my colleague commenting
(a bit too brusquely for my taste), "So, Irv, what's happening
is that you're not recording events."

Emily, who had been listening attentively, said, "Dr.
Yalom, that's one of the things I wanted to talk to you about.
I have been very worried about similar things. I'm especially
worried now about my problem recognizing faces. I'm terrified of developing Alzheimer's disease."

I responded quickly. "Let me offer you some reassurance
about that, Emily. Your condition, known as facial blind-
ness or prosopagnosia, is *not* a precursor to Alzheimer's. You
might be interested in reading some works by the wonderful
neurologist and writer, Oliver Sacks, who had facial recognition problems himself and has written brilliantly about it."

"I'll check that out. I'm familiar with him—he's a wonderful writer. I loved *The Man Who Mistook His Wife for a
Hat*. He's British, you know."

I nodded, "I'm a big fan of his. A couple of years ago
when he was fatally ill, I sent him a fan letter, and a couple
of weeks later, I received a note from his companion telling me he had read my note to Oliver Sacks just a few days
before he died. But let me tell you something else, Emily, I
have some personal experience with this condition. I notice it
most when I watch films or TV—I'm always asking my wife,
'Who's that person?' In fact I know that, without my wife,
I couldn't watch a great many films. I'm no expert in this

disorder and I think you should discuss it with a neurologist but, rest easy, it is *not* the sign of early dementia."

And so our session or, better, our intimate conversation, proceeded for fifty minutes. I can't be certain, but I suspected that sharing so much of myself was meaningful to her. For my part, I am certain I'll never forget our hour together because it was the time when I made the decision to retire from my life's work.

The following day Emily was still on my mind, and I sent her an email apologizing once more for being unprepared for our session and I expressed my hope that, even so, she might have derived benefit from our meeting. She responded the next day saying she was very moved by my apology and commented that she was grateful for all of our meetings. On reflection, she wrote, "It was your kind actions *between* meetings in the past that had especially moved me: lending me thirty dollars for a taxi to take me to the airport because I had no American money, once allowing me to give you a warm hug when we ended, refusing to accept payment for our last session, and now, a moving letter of apology. These are human being to human being: not so much therapist-client moments, and these moments have made a huge difference to me (and to my own clients). It is very heartening to know that even when we get it wrong (i.e., being human) we can make it right with authenticity and kindness."

I'll always be grateful to Emily for her letter. It neutralized so much of the sting of retirement.

CHAPTER 6

SETBACKS AND RENEWED HOPES

JUNE IS USUALLY A MONTH of family celebrations: Irv's birthday on June 13, Father's Day on June 21, and our wedding anniversary on June 27. This June should have been extra special—we were celebrating our sixty-fifth wedding anniversary! That makes us bona fide period pieces, since few Americans reach that milestone. People now marry so much later in life than in the past—that is, if they marry at all. We had planned a gala anniversary celebration on June 27, but have decided to put it off until I am presumably "better."

Last month, I went to a Bay Area support group for multiple myeloma patients that was held at Stanford and came away with new resolve to be more proactive concerning my disease. Though I admired the courage of the younger patients in taking on radical measures of treatment, such as stem cell and bone marrow transplants, I am not willing to go that route. I also wonder about the overuse of drugs and the "one-size fits-all" prescriptions that may have led to my stroke in February.

But it looks as if the decreased chemotherapy I have been receiving for the past month is not working, and I need to return to a higher dosage. I dread this change because the side effects were so severe in the past, and I do not want to suffer extensively in the little time I have remaining. For now, I am willing to see if the return to level 2 Velcade (one step below the highest dosage) will be sufficient to arrest the disease.

This has also been a very difficult time for Irv. Being a psychiatrist has been such an integral part of his identity, and he is grappling with the reality of retirement. He will severely miss his life as a therapist, yet I know Irv will find a way to maintain his professional identity. He answers scores of emails every day, still offers one-time consultations, and addresses audiences of therapists via Zoom. Most of all he is always writing something.

I worry equally about his physical state, especially his lack of balance which requires a cane in the house and a walker outdoors. It terrifies me to think that he might fall and severely injure himself.

We make a fine pair, I with myeloma and he with his heart and balance problems.

Two old people in the final dance of life.

———

On Father's Day, our children and grandchildren prepared a fabulous lunch for us out on the patio with some of Irv's favorite dishes: eggplant, mashed potatoes and parsnips, grilled chicken, salad, and chocolate cake. We are so lucky to have loving children who look after us and whom we can count upon. Like most parents, we hope our children will continue to be a "family" even after we are gone, but that, of course, will no longer be in our hands.

Right now, all the children and grandchildren are doing fine. Our eldest granddaughter, Lily, and her wife, Aleida, are happy in their marriage, have jobs, and recently bought a home in Oakland. I'm glad they are living in the Bay Area where same-sex marriage is generally accepted. Our second-oldest granddaughter, Alana, is in her last year of medical school at Tulane and is headed for a career in obstetrics/gynecology, like her mother. Lenore, our third granddaughter, will start graduate school in biology at Northwestern. Our eldest grandson, Jason, has completed college in Japan and is working for an architectural firm that specializes in overseas development. Desmond, our second grandson, has just graduated from Hendrix College in Arkansas with a degree in math and computer science. As a grandmother, I am happy to see them all launched professionally.

But it is difficult to accept that I will not be around to watch my three youngest grandchildren grow: 6-year-old Adrian, 3-year-old Maya, and 1-year-old Paloma, all born to Ben and Anisa. In Adrian's first years, he and I bonded over nursery rhymes. I read them to him and then he learned to recite and act them out. I see him in my mind's eye having a "great fall" like Humpty Dumpty or running off like the dish and the spoon in "Hey Diddle Diddle." Now that my life expectancy is short, it saddens me that I will not see Adrian, Maya, and Paloma as teenagers. They will not know me, except in flitting memories. Well, Adrian perhaps, whenever he hears a nursery rhyme.

———

Today, I go in for my Velcade injection. Irv takes me, of course, and, as always, stays with me through the procedure. First, I have blood drawn in the lab—always an efficient and generally painless procedure—and the lab results determine the exact amount of Velcade necessary to reach the proper dosage for someone of my height and weight. I feel reassured by this personalized approach, especially after my near-death stroke.

The Velcade injection is administered by a nurse in the Infusion Center. The nursing staff is extremely efficient and friendly. They answer all my questions, while seeing to it that I am covered with heated blankets and given apple juice to keep me hydrated. The injection is given in the flesh around the abdomen and lasts only a few seconds. For once, I am glad to have that extra band of flesh.

Afterwards, Irv and I go to the Stanford Shopping Center for lunch. I realize during lunch that I am actually taking pleasure in something! I hope the good feelings will continue.

———

Contrary to my worries, the aftereffects of the Velcade injection have not been severe. One of the reasons that the Velcade injection is not totally horrific has to do with the steroid pills I take before the treatment. They seem to make me less anxious and perkier than usual. Their only downside is that they also keep me awake at night, so I also resort to powerful sleeping pills.

One night, our neighbors Lisa and Herman come over to share a pizza. Lisa had been diagnosed with breast cancer ten years ago, and after an onslaught of treatment, including mastectomy, radiation, and chemotherapy, she has been in remission. It is validating to hear that she also experienced chemo brain and that she also had trouble sleeping on the days she took steroids with her chemo medication. Her experience makes my adverse symptoms seem "normal" and possibly ephemeral in the long run. Now, at 65, Lisa continues to lead a very good life distinguished by the energy and imagination she and her husband display in their work together as organizational psychologists.

I am able to sit at my computer, answer emails, and return to writing. I'm also selecting material for the Stanford archives, to which we have been giving papers and books for at least a decade. Irv has left this to me since he doesn't seem to care about what becomes of his papers. When Irv questions whether anyone will ever look at his archives, I remind him that two significant people already have consulted the archives: Sabine Gisiger for her film *Yalom's Cure* and Jeffrey Berman for his book on Irv's oeuvre entitled *Writing the Talking Cure*.

I tackle yet another drawer full of papers, and there is a constant ache in my heart to realize how much of the life we have lived will die with us. Papers in archives can only give clues to the nature of an existence. It is up to the researcher, historian, biographer, or filmmaker to bring life to materials so fastidiously preserved in library containers. Some of the documents, like two articles Irv and I wrote together on "Guilt" and "Widows," had been completely forgotten even by both of us. When and why did we write them? Were they ever published?

Some pieces of our past make me smile, for example, a 1998 letter from writer Tillie Olsen in her inimitable tiny handwriting. Tillie participated in a program of public interviews that I organized at Stanford, which were recorded in an edited book called *Women Writers of the West Coast* with superb photos by Margo Davis. Tillie could be impossible, and, at the same time, so brilliant. One day when she spoke in one of my Stanford classes, she looked around and commented: "There's nothing wrong with privilege. Everyone should have it."

Much of what I find can simply be thrown away. Who wants records collected from a hundred different American cemeteries? Still, it pains me to throw away those documents. Each represents a visit to a specific cemetery with my son Reid when we toured the US for our book *The American Resting Place*. Millions of people have erected tombstones over the remains of their family members. There is something comforting about a stone marked, presumably for eternity, with the name of your loved one. I am grateful that the book survives in print.

Sorting out one's papers can be a highly emotional experience for anyone, and in my case—having lived so fully in the realm of writing—it sometimes shakes me to the core. I am shocked to find a document entitled "What Matters to Me" written about ten years ago for a talk at Stanford. The content of the talk is so close to my current concerns:

> I woke up yesterday morning with the image of a four-leaf clover in my head. I knew immediately that it was related to my talk today. Dreams and waking images are often means for me to see deeper into myself . . . This

one was partially puzzling because I had already planned to speak about three things—represented by three of the four leaves—but I didn't know what the fourth leaf was supposed to represent . . .

1. What matters to me is my family and my close friends. In this way, I am like almost everyone else in the world . . .

2. What matters to me is my work, no longer as a professor, but as a writer reaching out to readers within and beyond the academic circle . . .

3. What matters to me is Nature, another form of beauty and truth. Throughout my life the natural world has been a source of enjoyment, comfort, and inspiration . . .

4. And now I remember what the fourth leaf of the clover represents. It has to do with the moral impulse, with the search for meaning and human connection, and with our relation to Nature, that we now lump together under the word "spirituality" . . .

There is no single directive for everyone; each must find what matters to him or to her. But along the way there are clues and signposts. I've learned to find my best self from many sources, written and unwritten: English and American poets, the Bible, Proust, Maxine Hong Kingston, the sight of a covey of quail, and the opening of a rose bud. I carry within me the memory of parents and teachers and colleagues, who were generous and loving. And I hold within my heart a line from the 23rd Psalm: "Surely goodness and mercy shall follow me all the days of my life." I try to be worthy of that line and to pass it on to the next generation. Now, as my time on earth draws to a close, I am trying to live out my remaining days in accordance with those principles.

———

Despite the setbacks, there are still moments when it's good to be alive. Close friends from Stanford and Marin County came for dinner recently, and I was able to share three hours with them. It certainly helped that David Spiegel, from the Stanford psychiatry department, and Michael Krasny, best known for his KQED radio show "Forum," are adept at telling Jewish jokes.

Now, when some of the unpleasant side effects of my illness return, I try to remember how much I laughed in the company of these loyal, witty friends. Recently, I discovered a prominent sty in my right eye. My eye doctor said I should treat it with hot compresses and antibiotic drops; he didn't think it was related to my disease. But now two more sties appear, and I begin to get worried. Irv looks up "sty and multiple myeloma" on the internet. Sure enough, sties are listed as a side effect of Velcade.

My internist and hematologist say I should continue with the hot compresses, but neither suggests abandoning the Velcade. So here I am again caught between the advantages of a life-prolonging drug and its unpleasant side effects. As one scientist put it in Katherine Eban's 2019 book *Bottle of Lies*, "All medicines are poisonous. It's only under the most controlled conditions that they do good." Or, as I realized all too well after the disaster caused by taking Revlimid, the chemo drug that precipitated my stroke: chemotherapy can prolong your life, that is, if it doesn't kill you first.

I wonder if I shall ever go into remission. Will this summer be my last?

I fall back on the words from Ecclesiastes: "There is a time for every season. . . . A time to be born and a time to die."

CHAPTER 7

STARING AT THE SUN, ONCE AGAIN

MARILYN AND I HAVE an important meeting with Dr. M., the oncology physician in charge of Marilyn's treatment. Dr. M. begins by agreeing that the side effects of the chemotherapy have been too severe for Marilyn to tolerate, and the laboratory results indicate that the chemotherapy at the lower dosage is ineffective. Hence, she suggests another route, an immunoglobulin approach, consisting of weekly infusions that would directly attack the cancer cells. She presents the important data: 40 percent of patients have significant side effects from the infusion—difficulties in breathing and rashes—most of which can be countered by strong antihistamines. Two-thirds of the patients who are able to tolerate the side effects experience great improvement. I'm unsettled by her message that if Marilyn is in the third of patients who are not helped by this approach, then there is no hope.

Marilyn agrees to the immunoglobulin approach, but never one to mince her words, poses a bold question: "If this route proves to be intolerable or ineffective, would you agree to my meeting with palliative care to discuss physician-assisted suicide?"

Dr. M. is startled and hesitates for a few seconds but then agrees to Marilyn's request and refers us to Dr. S., the head of palliative medicine. A few days later we meet with Dr. S., a reassuring, very perceptive, and gentle woman, who points out the many ways her department might be helpful in alleviating the side effects of the drugs Marilyn is taking. Marilyn listens patiently but eventually asks, "What role can palliative medicine play if I were in so much discomfort that I wished to end my life?"

Dr. S. hesitates a moment and then replies that, if two physicians agree in writing, they would assist her in ending her life. Marilyn seemed much calmed by this information and agrees to embark upon a month of the new immuno-globulin treatment.

I am stunned and sit there shaken but, at the same time, admiring Marilyn's directness and fearlessness. The options are diminishing, and we are now openly, almost casually, discussing Marilyn ending her life. I leave the session stunned and disoriented.

Marilyn and I spend the rest of the day close together: my first impulse is not to let her out of my sight, to stay near, to hold her hand and not let go. I fell in love with her seventy-three years ago, and we have just celebrated our sixty-fifth wedding anniversary. I know it is unusual to adore another person so much and for so long. But, even now, whenever she enters the room, I light up. I admire everything about her—her grace, her beauty, her kindness, and her wisdom. Though our intellectual backgrounds are different, we share a great love of literature and drama. Apart from the world of science, she is remarkably well informed. Any time I have a question about any aspect of the humanities, she rarely fails to edify me. Our relationship has not always been tranquil: we've had our differences, our quarrels, our indiscretions, but have always been forthright and honest with one another and always, always, put our relationship first.

We've spent almost our entire lives together, but now her diagnosis of multiple myeloma forces me to think about a life without her. For the first time, her death seems not only real, but close at hand. It's horrifying to imagine a world without Marilyn, and the thought of dying together with her passes through my mind. In the last few weeks, I've spoken about this to my closest physician friends. One of them shared that he, too, has considered suicide if his spouse were to die. Some of my friends would also consider suicide if they were facing severe dementia. We've even had conversations about methods, such as a large dose of morphine, certain antidepressants, helium, or other suggestions from the Hemlock Society.

In my novel, *The Spinoza Problem*, I write about Hermann Goring's last days at Nuremberg and describe how he cheated the hangman by swallowing a vial of cyanide somehow sequestered on his body. Cyanide capsules were distributed to all the top Nazis and many (Hitler, Goebbels, Himmler, Bormann) died in the same fashion. That was seventy-five years ago! What about now? Where can one get such a cyanide vial nowadays?

But I don't ponder such questions very long before the obvious dark consequences pop into view: the impact of my suicide upon my children and upon our entire network of friends. And upon my patients. I've worked for so many years in individual and group therapy with widows and widowers, and dedicated myself to keeping them alive through that excruciating first year, sometimes two years, after their spouse's death. So many times I've beamed with pleasure as I watched them gradually improve and reenter life. Ending my own life would be such a betrayal of their work, of our work. I helped them survive their pain and suffering and then, when faced with their situation, I choose to cop out. No, I cannot do that. Helping my patients is at the very core of my life: it is something I cannot and will not violate.

———

Several weeks have passed since my encounter with the Scottish patient that resulted in my decision to retire immediately from my work as a therapist. I continue to do single-session consultations, perhaps four or five weekly, but I no longer have ongoing patients. It's a great loss for me, having been a therapist for so long, I feel adrift without my work, and I search for a purposeful way of life. I can still write, and this joint project with Marilyn is an elixir of life, not only for her but for me as well. In my search for inspiration, I open a large old file entitled "notes for writing," containing ideas that I have jotted down over many decades.

The file is filled with narratives arising from my therapy with patients. The more I read, the more fascinated I become with all this good material for teaching young therapists. I have strong scruples about maintaining confidentiality. Even though this file is meant only for my eyes, I never use my patients' real names. So the more I perused, the more puzzled I grew. Who were these individuals I treated long ago? I had been far too successful in concealing their identities and could no longer recall their faces. Moreover, having believed that

my memory was indestructible, I made matters worse by failing to eliminate any material that I had already used in earlier
books. Had I the foresight to think of myself as a forgetful
old man in his late eighties rereading this file, I would have
made notations such as "used in 19xx or 20xx in such-and-
such book." Without such notations, a vexing problem arose:
Which stories of which clients had I already written about?
And in which book? I was in danger of plagiarizing myself.

Without question, rereading some of my own books is
called for: I hadn't read any of them for a great many years.
When I turn to the bookshelf containing my works, the
glaring yellow book jacket of *Staring at the Sun* catches my
eye. It is a relatively recent book, written about fifteen years
ago in my early seventies. The central thesis of the book is
that death anxiety plays a far greater role in the lives of our
patients than has generally been acknowledged. Now, closer
to the end of my own life and with my wife facing a mortal
illness and contemplating suicide, I wonder how the book
will strike me now. For so many years, I've struggled to
comfort my patients who were wrestling with death anxiety.
Now my turn has come. Can *Staring at the Sun* help me?
Can I find comfort in my own words?

An odd passage toward the beginning of the book catches
my eye—words by Milos Kundera, one of my favorite writers.
"*What terrifies most about death is not the loss of the future but
the loss of the past. In fact, the act of forgetting is a form of death
always present within life.*"

That thought has immediate meaning. It rings ever more
true as I grow aware of important chunks of my past disap-
pearing from my memory. Marilyn shields me from this by
her astounding recall. But when she's not available, I am

staggered by the holes in my memory. I realize that, when she dies, a great deal of my past will die with her. A few days ago, as she was going over material to place into the Stanford University archives, she came across the syllabus for a course entitled "Death in Life and Literature" that she and I taught together at Stanford in 1973. She wanted to reminisce about the course, but I couldn't truly join her: it has entirely vanished from my mind. I recall none of our lectures nor any faces of our students.

So, yes, Kundera nailed it: "*the act of forgetting is a form of death always present within life.*"

I can feel the pangs of sadness when I think of my vanished past. I am the sole holder of memories of so many dead individuals—my father and mother, my sister, so many playmates and friends and patients of long ago, who now exist as only flickering impulses in my nervous system. I alone keep them alive.

In my mind's eye, I see my father so clearly. It is a Sunday morning, and as always, we are sitting at our red leather table playing chess. He was a handsome man and combed his long black hair straight back without a part. I imitated his hair style until I entered junior high school when my mother and sister nixed it. I recall winning most of our chess games, but even now I don't know whether my father purposely let me win. I recall his kind face for a few moments. Then his image fades, and he returns to oblivion. How sad to think that when I die, he will vanish forever. There will be no one else alive who remembers his face. This thought—the transient nature of the entire world of experience—makes me shiver.

I remember once telling my therapist and, later, my friend Rollo May about remembering those chess games with my father. Rollo said that he hoped I would keep *him* alive in the same fashion. He commented that much of anxiety stems back to the fear of oblivion and that "*anxiety about nothing tries to become anxiety about something.*" In other words, anxiety about nothingness quickly attaches itself to a tangible, concrete object.

I feel gratified by readers who email and tell me how much my books have moved and influenced them. Yet, lurking in my mind is the knowledge that everything—all memory, all influence—is transient. In a generation, perhaps two at best, no one will read my books or think of me. Certainly no one will have memories of me as a material being. Not to know this, not to accept the evanescence of existence, is to live in self-deception.

An early chapter in *Staring at the Sun* deals with the "awakening experience," an experience that awakens one to mortality. I've written at length about Scrooge in Dickens's *A Christmas Carol*, who was visited by the ghost of "Christmas Yet to Come." The ghost offers Scrooge a preview of his death and the ensuing uninterested reaction of all who had known him. Awakened to the selfish and solipsistic manner in which he has lived, Scrooge undergoes a major and positive personality transformation. Another well-known awakening experience occurs to Tolstoy's Ivan Ilyich who, on his deathbed, realizes that he was dying so badly because he had lived badly. Acquiring that knowledge, even at the very end of his life, catalyzes a major transformation.

I have witnessed the impact of such life experiences in many of my patients. But I am uncertain whether I have personally experienced such a singular dramatic awakening experience. If so, it has vanished from memory. In my medical training, I can recall no patients who died under my care. Nor had I, or any of my closest friends, come close to death. Even so, I have frequently thought about death—my death—a great deal, and I assumed that my concerns were universal.

When I decided that psychotherapy was to be my life's work and began my psychiatric residency at Johns Hopkins in 1957, I was disappointed and puzzled by my first exposure to psychoanalytic thought, especially in its inattention to deeper issues linked to mortality. During my first year of training, I was intrigued by Rollo May's new book, *Existence*. I read it avidly from cover to cover and understood that the work of many existential philosophers was highly relevant to my field. I concluded that it was imperative for me to obtain an education in philosophy, and during my second year of residency, I assiduously attended a year-long undergraduate course in Western philosophy, meeting thrice weekly in the evenings at the Hopkins undergraduate campus on the opposite side of Baltimore from the hospital and our residence. This course deepened my appetite for philosophy, and I read widely in that field. When I came to Stanford years later, I attended many philosophy courses, and remain friends to this day with my two favorite teachers, Dagfin Follesdal and Van Harvey.

In my first years as a therapist, I took note of awakening experiences reported by my patients. In *Staring at the Sun*, I describe one of my long-term patients whose husband died

in the midst of our therapy. Shortly afterwards, she made the
decision to move from the large house where she had raised her
children into a small two-room apartment. Again and again,
she was chagrinned at giving away items saturated with memories of her husband and children, knowing that strangers would
use these items while being unaware of the stories associated
with each of them. I recall feeling extraordinarily close to her.
I imagined being in her position. I had known her deceased
husband, a Stanford professor, and I could feel her pain as she
had to part with so many reminders of their life together.

I began exploring paths to bring the confrontation with
death into psychotherapy when I was a faculty member at
Stanford. I treated a great many patients who had a fatal
illness and began considering leading a therapy group for
such individuals. One memorable day, Katie W., a remarkable woman with metastatic cancer, entered my office, and
through her contacts with the American Cancer Association,
she and I organized a therapy group program for patients
who were dying of metastatic cancer. I and several of my students and colleagues led such groups for many years. Though
these groups are common today, in 1970 this was, to the best
of my knowledge, the first such group offered anywhere. It
was in this group that I had my first unforgettable exposures
to death as, one by one, the members of my groups died
from their cancer.

During this experience, my own anxiety about death
rocketed, and I decided to enter therapy once again. By
sheer coincidence Rollo May had moved from New York to
California and opened an office at his Tiburon home about
an eighty-minute drive from Stanford. I contacted him, and
we met weekly for the next two years. He was helpful to me

although I believe that, more than once, my discussions of death took its toll on him. (He was twenty-two years older.) After our treatment ended, he and I, his wife Georgia, and Marilyn all became close friends. Years later, Georgia phoned to say that Rollo was dying and asked Marilyn and me to come to their house. We rushed over to sit vigil with Georgia by his bedside, and Rollo died about two hours after our arrival. It's strange how lucidly I recall every detail of that evening. Death has a way of catching your attention and etching itself permanently into your memory.

———

I continue reading *Staring at the Sun* and come upon a discussion of school and college reunions, which always increase one's awareness of aging and, inevitably, death. It brings to mind an event that took place only two months earlier.

I attended a memorial luncheon for David Hamburg, the former chairman of psychiatry at Stanford. I cared deeply about David: he offered me my first, and only, academic position and became an important mentor and model to me. My expectation was that the memorial luncheon would be a reunion, and I would see all my old colleagues and friends from the Stanford psychiatry faculty. Though there was a large crowd at the event, only two members of the early department of psychiatry were in attendance. They were both quite aged—but both had joined the department many years after I had come to Stanford. How disappointing: I had so hoped to have a reunion with the dozen Young Turks who had joined the department with me fifty-seven years ago, when the fledgling medical school first opened in Palo Alto.

(Up to that time the Stanford Medical School had been located in San Francisco.)

After milling about at the memorial luncheon, conversing, asking about old colleagues, I realized that, aside from me, every single one of the Young Turks was dead. I was the only one still alive! I tried to bring them to mind—Pete, Frank, Alberta, Betty, Gig, Ernie, two Davids, two Georges. I visualized most of their faces, but some names had slipped away. We had all been such young, bright, starry-eyed psychiatrists, all full of hope and ambition, all just beginning our careers.

I cannot help marveling at the power of denial. Again and again, I forget how old I am, and I forget that my early peers and friends are all dead, and that I am next in line. I continue to identify with the young boyish me until some stark confrontation yanks me back to reality.

I continue reading, and a passage on page 49 of *Staring at the Sun* catches my attention. I describe interviewing a grieving patient, who had lost a dear friend and developed disabling death anxiety.

"What do you most fear about death?" I asked.

She answered, "All the things I would not have done."

That feels extraordinarily important; it has been core to my therapy work. For many years, I have been convinced that there is a positive correlation between death anxiety and the sense of unlived life. In other words: the more unlived your life, the greater your death anxiety.

———

Few things confront us with mortality as strongly as the death of the significant other. In an early section of *Staring at the Sun*, I describe a patient's horrendous nightmare a few days after her husband's death. "I am on the screened porch of a flimsy summer cottage porch and am terrorized by a large menacing beast. I attempted to appease him by tossing him a doll dressed in red plaid. The beast devoured the doll but continued to fix his eyes on me." The meaning of the dream was crystal clear. Her husband had died wearing red plaid pajamas, and the dream tells her that death is implacable: her husband's death was not sufficient. She was also the beast's prey.

My wife's illness means that she will, in all probability, die before I do. But my turn will come soon thereafter. Strangely, I feel no terror about my death. Instead my terror stems from the thought of life without Marilyn. Yes, I know that the research, some of it my own work, informs us that grief is finite, that once we go through the events of one year—the four seasons, the birthdays and death days, the holidays, the entire twelve months—then our pain diminishes. By the time we go through the annual cycle twice, almost all of us will once again rejoin life. That's what I've written, but I doubt it will work in that manner for me. I've loved Marilyn since I was 15, and without her, I cannot imagine being entirely able to rejoin life. My life has been fully lived. All my ambitions have been satisfied. My four children and eldest grandchildren are all fully launched. I'm no longer indispensable.

One night I am particularly disturbed by dreams about Marilyn's death. I remember only one detail: I was strenuously expressing my dissatisfaction at being buried next to Marilyn (long ago we had purchased two adjoining plots). Instead I wanted us to be closer, to be buried in the same coffin! When I tell Marilyn about this in the morning, she informs me that it is not possible. Years ago, she and my photographer son, Reid, had visited cemeteries all over the United States for their book. In all of her research, she never encountered a coffin for two.

CHAPTER 8

WHOSE DEATH IS THIS ANYWAY?

I JUST READ IRV'S CHAPTER on rereading *Staring at the Sun*. I am moved and unsettled. He is already grieving my demise. How odd that I should be the one who will probably die first, when statistically it is more frequently the husband who dies first. Even the English language reveals the expected difference between genders. "Widower" for the husband has at its root the word "widow" for the wife. More typically, when there are two gendered forms for the same word, the root is masculine, "hero/heroine" or "poet/poetess." But here the feminine root speaks for the statistical prevalence of women outliving their spouses.

I cannot think ahead to Irv's widowerhood. It saddens me greatly to imagine him alone, but my focus remains, as it has for the past eight months, on my own physical condition. The months of chemotherapy that almost killed me and the devastating side effects of that second medication, Velcade, have taken their toll. Now, my new immunoglobular regime is less debilitating and, at times, allows me a few moments of pleasure with Irv, my children, grandchildren, and friends who come to visit. But who knows if this treatment will be effective?

We have already met with Dr. S., the Stanford head of palliative care, a lovely woman who has the huge responsibility of aiding patients at the end of their lives. If I am told by Dr. M. that the immunoglobulin treatment isn't working, I believe I shall opt for palliative care and, eventually, assisted suicide. I do not want to undergo any more dramatic measures. But will that decision be mine alone?

———

When our dear friends Helen and David bring us dinner, I tell them that palliative care and assisted suicide would be a relief if my present treatment is not effective.

David quickly retorts, "Your body has only one vote."

It occurs to me, as it has many times this year, that my death is not mine alone. I shall have to share it with those who love me, first of all with Irv, but also with other family members and close friends. Even though my circle of friends has always been important to me, I am surprised by the depth of concern that many of them have demonstrated once they hear the news of my illness. How fortunate for me to be surrounded by such caring people!

When the list of phone calls and emails became too numerous for me to answer individually, I took a bold step and wrote a collective email to about fifty friends. This is the message:

Dear friends,

Please forgive me for sending you this collective letter

instead of individual messages. I am grateful to each of you for your words of encouragement during these past six months—for your visits, cards, flowers, food, and other expressions of affection. Without the support of family and friends, I would never have made it this far.

For various reasons, we are now abandoning the chemo treatment and starting something new called immunoglobular therapy, which doesn't have the devastating side effects of chemo, but which is perhaps less effective. We shall know if it is working in a month or two.

If and when I am in better shape, I hope to contact each of you individually and set up time for a phone call or visit. In the meantime, please know that your thoughts and, in some cases, prayers gladden my heart and sustain me as I work with the Stanford medical team to prolong my life.

Sending love to each of you,
Marilyn

I feel a little awkward about having sent such a collective letter. Still, given the numerous responses I received, I'm glad I did: they give me additional reasons for trying to stay alive.

I think of my French diplomat friend, who has a very debilitating disease. He once said to me that he was not afraid of death (*la mort*) but that he certainly feared dying (*mourir*). I, too, am not afraid of death itself, but the process of dying in daily doses is often intolerable. For months now, I have been accustoming myself to the idea of my upcoming death. Since Irv and I have contemplated the subject of death for decades, both in our joint teaching and in his writing, I seem able to confront the idea with a degree of calm that surprises my friends. Sometimes I wonder if the calm is only a veneer and that underneath, I, too, am terrified.

Recently my well of hidden anguish spilled over into a vivid dream. In it, I am talking on the phone to a friend, and she tells me that her adult son has died the day before. I start to scream and awake convulsing with tears.

In real life, that friend does not even have a son.

So, whose death am I crying about? Probably my own.

CHAPTER 9

FACING ENDINGS

MARILYN AND I ARRIVE at the clinic at 8 A.M. for immunoglobulin therapy. I sit by her side for nine hours as the
medication is delivered via a slow IV drip. I watch her care-
fully, dreading a strong reaction to the drug. But I am elated
to see that she remains comfortable, has no negative reaction
to the medication, and sleeps much of her stay in the clinic.

Once home, the evening that follows is heavenly. We
watch the first episode of an old BBC series, *Martin Chuzzlewit*, with Paul Scofield. We are both Dickens lovers (especially me—she always places Proust first). For many years,
whenever traveling in the US or abroad to give a lecture, I
spent some of my free time visiting antiquarian bookstores,
from which I gradually have built up a large collection of
Dickens first editions.

As we watch the TV production, I am mesmerized by
the amazing cast of characters. But, alas, there are so many
characters introduced at once that my problems with facial

recognition leave me bewildered. I could not possibly watch the program without Marilyn identifying who is who. After we turn off the TV, Marilyn goes into the living room and fetches the first part of *Martin Chuzzlewit*. (Dickens's major novels were all published in twenty parts. Once each month a part was released and delivered by a huge fleet of yellow carts to enormous crowds eager to buy the new installment).

Marilyn opens the first part and, with much animation, begins reading aloud. As I lean back in my chair, holding her free hand, I purr in ecstasy, listening to each word. This is sheer heaven: what a blessing to have a wife who delights in reading Dickens's prose aloud. A magic moment for me, one of a vast number of such moments she has given me since we were adolescents.

———

But I know this is but a short respite from the dark task of facing mortality, and the following day I continue searching for help in the pages of *Staring at the Sun* and arrive at my discussion of Epicurus (341–270 BC), who offered nonreligious believers like me three lucid and powerful arguments to alleviate death anxiety. The first argument states that since the soul is mortal and perishes with the body, we will have no consciousness and therefore nothing to fear after death. The second states that, since the soul is mortal and dispersed at death, we have nothing to fear. Hence, "Where death is, I am not. Why fear something we can never perceive?"

Both of these seem obvious and offer some comfort, but it is Epicurus's third argument that always had the strongest appeal to me. It posits that one's state of nothingness after death is identical to the state of nothingness that one was in before birth.

A few pages later, I encounter my description of "rippling"—the idea that one's deeds and ideas ripple on to others, much like the ripples created by tossing a pebble into a pond. That thought, too, is enormously important to me. When I give something to my clients, I know that in some way they will, in turn, find a way to pass my gift to others, and on and on the ripples continue. This theme has been inherent in my work ever since I started practicing psychotherapy over sixty years ago.

Today I do not suffer excessively from death anxiety, that is, anxiety about my own death. My real anguish issues from the idea of losing Marilyn forever. Sometimes, for a moment, I have a flash of resentment that she has the privilege of dying first. It seems so much easier that way.

I stay constantly by her side. I hold her hand as we fall asleep. I take care of her in every possible way. And in these last months I rarely let an hour pass without leaving my office and walking the 120 feet to the house to see her. I don't often allow myself to think about my own death, but for the sake of this book I will set my imagination free. When I shall be facing death, there will be no Marilyn hovering, always available, always beside me. There will be no one holding my hand. Yes, my four children and my eight grandchildren and many friends will spend time with me, but alas, they will not have the power to penetrate the depths of my isolation.

I try to deal with the loss of Marilyn by thinking of all that I have lost and what will remain. I have no doubt that when Marilyn dies she will take much of my past life with her, and that thought leads to distress. Of course, I've visited many places without Marilyn—lectures, workshops, and many snorkeling or scuba excursions, my army trips to the Orient, my Vipassana retreat in India—but much of the memory of these experiences has already faded. We recently watched a film, *Tokyo Story*, and Marilyn reminded me of our trip to Tokyo, when we saw many of the buildings and parks shown in the film. I remembered none of them.

"Remember," she reminded me, "you consulted for three or so days at the Kurosawa Hospital and afterwards we visited Kyoto?"

Yes, yes, now it all began to drift back into my mind—the lectures I gave, the demonstration of a therapy group with the staff taking the role of patients, the wonderful parties thrown for us. But without Marilyn, it's unlikely I would have recalled any of it. Losing so much of my life when I still live—that is a truly frightening thing. Without her, the islands, the beaches, the friends in cities all over the world, much of the wonderful trips we've taken together will vanish aside from a few bleached memories.

I continue browsing in *Staring at the Sun* and come to a section I had entirely forgotten. It is an account of final meetings with two important mentors: John Whitehorn and Jerome Frank, both professors of psychiatry at Johns Hopkins. When I was a young faculty member at Stanford, I was much surprised by a call from John Whitehorn's daughter. She told me her father had had a severe stroke and that he had asked to see me before he died. I had much admired John Whitehorn—he was my teacher—and I had had professional contact with him. But we never, not once, had a personal encounter. He was always stiff and formal, it was always Doctor Whitehorn and Doctor Yalom. I never heard anyone, other faculty members, even chairs of other departments, refer to him by his first name.

Why me? Why would he ask to see me, a student with whom he had never shared an intimate moment? But I was so moved that he remembered me and had asked to see me that, a few hours later, I was on an airplane to Baltimore where I took a taxi directly to the hospital. When I entered his room, Dr. Whitehorn recognized me but was agitated and confused. Again and again he whispered softly, "I'm so damned scared." I felt helpless and wished so much I could have offered some help. I entertained the thought of hugging him, but no one hugged John Whitehorn. Then, about twenty minutes after I arrived, he fell unconscious. Full of sadness, I left the hospital. I assumed that in some manner I had meant something to him, perhaps as a replacement for his own son who had died during World War II. I remember his plaintive look as he told me that his son had died in the Battle of the Bulge, and then he added, "That God-damned meat grinder."

My last visit to Jerome Frank, my major mentor at Johns Hopkins, was significantly different. In the last few months of his life, Jerry Frank suffered from severe dementia, and I visited him at a residential facility in Baltimore. I saw him sitting and looking out the window, and brought a chair to sit next to him. He was a lovely, kind man, and I always took delight in his presence. I asked him what his life was like now. "Every day a new day," he answered, "I wake up and, whoosh." He ran his hand over his forehead. "Yesterday's all gone. But I sit in this chair and watch life go by. It's not so bad, Irv. It's not so bad."

That hit home for me. I had long feared dementia more than death. But, now, Jerry Frank's words, "it's not so bad, Irv," startled and moved me. My old mentor was saying, "Irv, you, as you, have only this one life. Enjoy every part of this amazing phenomenon called 'consciousness' and don't drown yourself in remorse for what you once had!" His words have power and temper my terror of dementia.

Another passage from *Staring at the Sun* also offers succor. In a section entitled "Love Bliss," I discuss how a starry-eyed infatuation pushes all other concerns off the table. Watch how an agitated child climbs into his mother's lap and is quickly soothed as all troublesome concerns evaporate. I described this as "the lonely 'I' dissolving into the 'we.'" The pain of isolation evaporates. This really strikes home for me. A near lifetime of being in love with Marilyn has, without doubt, shielded me from experiencing the deep loneliness of isolation, and a goodly part of my current pain arises from anticipated solitude.

I imagine my life after Marilyn's death, and I picture night after night spent alone in my large empty house. I have many friends and children and grandchildren, even one great grandchild, and attentive kind neighbors, but they lack Marilyn's magic. The task of enduring such fundamental solitude seems overwhelming. Then I take solace again in Jerry Frank's words, "I sit in this chair and watch life go by. It's not so bad, Irv."

CHAPTER 10

CONSIDERING PHYSICIAN-ASSISTED SUICIDE

I GO FOR MY THIRD immunoglobulin treatment at the Stanford Hospital. Irv accompanies me at 11:00 and stays with me till 5:00, except for a couple of hours that he takes off for lunch and a rest. During that time, my dear friend Vida comes to sit with me and gives me comfort. She has been more than attentive during my illness, visiting often and bringing tasty food that is easy on the stomach. Today she brings me chicken, rice, and cooked carrots.

Oddly enough, the day I spend at the hospital is one of my easiest days of the week, with no attendant bad side effects. The staff are invariably courteous, knowledgeable, and efficient. I lie down on a comfortable bed and receive a drug dosage that drips slowly into my body. When I leave, I feel rested and in good spirits, most likely due to the steroids given before the intravenous drip starts.

As we leave the hospital, I am moved by the thought that our "baby" son, Ben, was born in another wing of this hospital almost exactly fifty years ago. Tomorrow, he, his wife Anisa, and their three children will arrive to celebrate Ben's fiftieth birthday with us. We've already made up the extra beds in Irv's study and mine, and I shall do all I can not to look like a dying old lady to my grandchildren.

Ben's family spends the weekend with us. On Saturday, we throw a party in the nearby park to celebrate Ben's birthday. Even though invitations went out only a week ago, most of his friends are there. A few of them had known Ben in elementary school, others in high school and college, and some from his summers at Camp Tawonga in the Sierras. It is a pleasure to see these "boys"—now middle-aged men with wives and children of their own, ranging from toddlers to teenagers. Ben always had a great capacity for friendship, and I'm happy to see that he and his friends have continued to be loyal to each other.

My strongest pleasure, of course, is spending time with Ben and Ani's children: Adrian at 6, Maya at 3, and Paloma at 1. The little girls are as sweet as can be, and Adrian, when he's not having a tantrum, is a real charmer. He has the advantage—or perhaps the disadvantage—of being extremely beautiful, having inherited his mother's widely spaced blue eyes, her fair hair, and a face shaped like an angel's. On top of that, he's very intelligent and articulate. But when he is seized by one of his fits, he turns into a proverbial devil. I'm amazed at his parents' patience with him and their hard-tried belief supported by the best psychiatric advice that he will eventually outgrow his objectionable behavior. Before they leave, Adrian kisses me good-bye and says, "I think I'll see you at Thanksgiving." At the back of my mind, I wonder what kind of shape I'll be in at Thanksgiving. I wonder if I'll be here at all.

The day they leave, I get sick again with the old demons of nausea and loose bowels, probably due to the food I let myself eat at Ben's party. When that happens, I feel so miserable that I wish I could just exit this life peacefully without further suffering. My concerns for other people take a nosedive, even my sadness at the thought of never seeing my loved ones again.

Eventually, with anti-nausea medication, I get the physical situation under control, but my fears do not go away and find expression in a terrifying nap-time dream. I am on the phone with a colleague who, in real life, has had several bouts of breast cancer. She and I are working on a project together, the files for which I attempt to find in my computer. I keep pressing different titles but cannot bring up anything resembling our project. At one point, I hit an icon on my desktop computer and, instead of a file, I get an auditory response so deafening that I could not hear my colleague's voice at the other end of the line. The noise just gets louder and louder, and there is no way to turn off the sound. I panic and try to pull out the computer cord, but even that doesn't work. The noise seems to be coming from everywhere. I run through the house to all the other outlets, screaming as I go, "Help me, help me unplug the cords."

It doesn't take my psychiatrist husband long to analyze the dream and see in it my desire to end an agonizing life.

———

Irv takes me again to the hospital for my weekly immuno-globin infusion. Everything goes very smoothly, including the long nap I have as a result of the Benadryl taken as part of the pretreatment medication. When I awake, Irv is sitting by my side and asks how I feel. Usually I say something like "okay" or "so so" in order spare him my wretchedness. But today, in light of our upcoming meeting tomorrow with Dr. M., I decide to be franker than usual.

"Well, if you are up to hearing the truth, I've felt for a long time that I'm paying too great a cost to stay alive. I've had nine months of chemotherapy and now immunoglobulin treatment, and the toll taken on my body has changed me. I awake each morning and after each nap with an aversion to getting up. How much longer must I live before I am allowed to die?"

"But sometimes you enjoy yourself—like when we sit together outdoors holding hands or watch the television at night."

"Enjoy . . . *c'est beaucoup dire*. If I'm not truly wretched with stomach problems, I tolerate my physical condition and am glad to be with you. You are the main reason I have for staying alive. You know, when I was first diagnosed with multiple myeloma, the smiling doctors told me that people can live for years with the disease, that is, if they respond positively to chemotherapy and other forms of treatment. They did not say that I was dying and that the treatments would extract a permanent toll on my body. Gradually I came to the understanding that I would never be the same again—that I would pass through days of unspeakable misery, while my body would decline and weaken. If I could place you inside my body for just a few minutes, you would understand."

Irv was silent for a long time. Then he countered, "Isn't it enough that you are still alive? That when you go, there will be nothing afterwards? And I'm not ready to let you go."

"Irv, during these past nine months, I think I've come to terms with death. After all, I'm 87 years old and I've had a great life. If I were 40 or 50 or 60, then it would be a tragedy, but now, for me, death is an inevitable reality. Whether I die in three months or longer, I think I can accept the fact. Yes, of course, I shall be sad to leave my loved ones, especially you."

There are two things from Irv's writing that have been influential in how I now see death. The first is what he's written about the unlived life. I am one of the lucky ones who will die with no regrets, thus should have an easier time facing death. Certainly, I feel nothing but gratitude for Irv, my children, my friends, the Stanford doctors, and the material circumstances that make it possible to live my last days in comfortable surroundings.

The second thing from Irv's writing that keeps circling in my head is Nietzsche's phrase "Die at the right time." That's what I'm grappling with right now. What is the right time for me to die? Does it make sense for me to prolong my life if it means continuing to live with so much physical wretchedness? What if Dr. M. tells us that the immunoglobulin treatment is not working? What if she proposes some other treatment? Here's how I would react to that: I would choose to let the palliative doctors take over and help me die as painlessly as possible. And I would ask for assisted suicide.

It seems to me that the decision to live or die should be primarily mine. And I'm beginning to feel that the "right time to die" is not a hypothetical period of months and years into the future, but sooner rather than later. I have even begun to detach myself from objects and people. Last time our granddaughter, Lily, visited, I gave her something I loved—a page from a medieval manuscript bought on the quays in Paris when I was a student there. I gave Alana a very special jacket she had admired long ago. And I gave Anisa a silver necklace with a heart carrying tiny diamonds. It looked so lovely on her.

But even more than that, I am trying to detach myself a little from the people I love most. It was good to see Ben's kids recently, to feel that they are going to be fine. Yet I don't want to be worrying too much about them or any of the family—Irv is the only one I need to be thinking about. Of course, a lot depends on what Dr. M. has to say, but I know I will have to ask Irv not to put too much pressure on me to share his view that it is worth staying alive at all costs.

September

CHAPTER 11

A TENSE COUNTDOWN
TO THURSDAY

EACH WEDNESDAY I sit for long hours by Marilyn's hospital bedside hoping that she will tolerate the intravenous infusion. Much to my surprise and relief, she has had no immediate negative reactions to the drug, and our Wednesdays have been fairly peaceful. Each week on arrival at the center, Marilyn has blood drawn, and we wait an hour until the lab results determine her dosage that day. Then, in a small private room, her IV is started and Marilyn soon falls asleep. I sit by her bed for four to six hours, reading the newspapers, doing email on my laptop, and reading a novel on my iPad. (Thomas Hardy's _Tess of the d'Urbervilles_ so engrosses me that the hours zoom by.)

On this Wednesday, I decide to visit the Lane Medical Library while Marilyn sleeps. I hoped to read some recent issues of psychiatry journals—something, I'm embarrassed to admit, I had not done for far too long. I remember spending a great many hours in the Lane Library over a period of forty years whilst a faculty member of the Stanford Psychiatry

Department, and recalled with pleasure the vast journal reading room where recent issues of countless medical journals
were displayed and read by a great many medical students,
house staff, and faculty.

I am told that the library is only a short ten-minute walk
through the hospital. Lane Library in the Stanford Medical
School is contiguous with the Stanford Hospital. Marilyn's
attending nurse points out the general direction to the library, and I saunter off. But nothing in the hospital is the
same: I am immediately lost and ask directions several times
until someone wearing an official badge takes pity on this
old geezer with a cane, wandering unsteadily through the
passages of the hospital aisles, and he personally guides me to
the library. Even so, we have to stop at check points before
each ward, where I must show my faculty card to guards.

After presenting my ID card at the library, I enter, pleas-
antly anticipating my return to the old familiar reading room.
But that was not to be: *there was no reading room.*

Instead I see only rows and rows of desks occupied by
individuals staring at computers. I look about for a librarian.
There used to be a great many librarians assisting library users,
but I see nary a one—until I spot an official-looking dour
woman in a far corner of the room bent over a computer.

I walk over to her and posed my question, "Can you di-
rect me to the reading room? When I was last here—quite a
while ago, I admit—it occupied much of this first floor area
and displayed the most recent editions of dozens of journals.
I'm looking for some current psychiatry journals."

She seems befuddled and stares at me as though I were a
creature from another century (which of course I am). "We
don't have paper journals here. They're all online."

"You mean to tell me that, in this entire medical library, there is not a single paper copy of a recent psychiatry journal?"

With her face still scrunched in confusion, she replies, "Perhaps I may have seen one on the floor below," and then abruptly turns her attention back to her computer.

Wandering downstairs, I again see nothing but individuals hunched over computer screens. At the back of the room, however, I spot the huge stacks of old bound journals. I find the section containing the *Journal of the American Psychiatric Association*, but the shelves are too close to one another to enter the aisle. A couple of minutes pass before I make a great "aha" discovery: the shelves are movable. I push hard enough for the stack to slide back and when there is sufficient room in the aisle, I enter the narrow aisle and begin searching for the bound psychiatric journals. Just then I hear voices and the ominous movement of shelves rolling. I recall that, on entering the stacks, I had seen (but ignored) a large sign saying: FOR YOUR SAFETY: LOCK ROLLERS.

Suddenly the meaning of that sign dawns on me, and I realize that I could be crushed and have to get the hell out of there. I scuttle out of the stacks and—with the help of another courteous hospital guide—make my return to Marilyn. I rarely venture far from her bedside again.

———

In addition to her medication, Marilyn is given steroids on Wednesdays that help her tolerate the weekly infusion and offer her comfort for the next forty-eight hours. But by Fridays, without fail, she develops unpleasant symptoms, including nausea, diarrhea, shivering, and great fatigue. These four weeks of treatment have passed very slowly, and I feel unable to focus on anything other than Marilyn and our future visit with the oncologist. I feel tense and depressed. I continually marvel that Marilyn has handled it so well. Her condition varies from day to day. On one occasion, I had just returned from grocery shopping when I heard her calling out to me from her usual perch on the living room sofa. She was visibly shivering and asked for warm blankets, which I promptly fetched. Two hours later she felt better and had a small supper of her usual food, chicken soup and apple juice.

As our Thursday meeting approaches, I grow uncertain of what Dr. M. had really said. What I recalled was that at least a third of patients were unable to tolerate the new treatment. The good news, of course, is that Marilyn had passed this hurdle. Then, to the best of my recall, Dr. M. had said that, of the remaining patients, two-thirds would have a positive result. But what of the one-third who did not respond? What did she say about those? Was it implicit that there were no remaining options for treatment? I recall that I had refrained from posing that question in Marilyn's presence.

By Tuesday evening, two days before our meeting, my anxiety grows. I phone my daughter, Eve, and my colleague and friend David Spiegel MD, who had both also attended the last meeting with Dr. M., and ask them what they remember of the discussion. They do *not* recall Dr. M. saying that if this treatment failed there were no remaining options, but they did recall that Marilyn interrupted Dr. M. and said that she would not undergo another form of treatment and would request palliative care.

Throughout all this travail, Marilyn remains calm on the outside, much calmer than I, and often she attempts to assuage my worry about her illness. But over and over, Marilyn speaks about physician-assisted suicide. *You just can't request physician-assisted suicide when there are effective treatments available*, I think, but do not want to hammer her with reality. She will learn this for herself. I keep reminding her of all the precious moments she is still experiencing. The fun we had the other night searching the TV apps for a good Japanese film with our granddaughter, Lenore. Our precious moments simply holding hands. "Think of these moments," I then say to her, "think of how blessed we are to experience this precious consciousness. I love every minute of it; we'll never have another shot at it. How can you just toss it away?"

"You're not listening" she replies. "I realize the preciousness of consciousness, but I cannot get through to you about how miserable I feel so much of the time. You've never experienced this. If not for you, I'd have found a way to end it long ago."

I listen. Is she right?

I think back to the times when I felt such misery. The worst was decades ago when we returned from a trip to the Bahamas, where I had picked up some tropical infection that floored me for months. I saw the best tropical medical experts but to no avail. I often had vertigo, felt nauseated, and spent weeks in bed. Ultimately, I joined a gym, found a trainer, and forced myself into recovery after six months of illness. But during all that time I never once contemplated suicide, I told Marilyn. I trusted my illness would pass and life was too precious. For years afterwards I was plagued by bouts

of postural vertigo—an awful experience—but somehow I
got through that and I've had no vertigo for many years. But
it's foolish to compare my illness with hers. Marilyn may be
right, maybe I underestimate the extent of her agony. I've
got to keep trying to experience life from her viewpoint.

———

Thursday finally arrives—the day of our meeting with Dr.
M. in which we will learn if Marilyn's immunoglobulin therapy is working. Because I am losing faith in my ability to
listen accurately, I ask our close friends David Spiegel and
his wife, Helen Blau, to accompany us. The meeting is a
disappointment—part of the necessary lab work had not yet
been done. There are two laboratory markers which would
inform us about Marilyn's response to treatment. One marker
was slightly positive, and the other lab marker had not yet
been ordered.

I pose a couple of questions to Dr. M. and say that I
had been very tense awaiting this session, expecting to learn
whether immunoglobulin was or was not working for Marilyn. Was I correct in expecting this information today?

Dr. M. says that I was indeed correct, that she had erred
in not ordering the laboratory study and will do that immediately. After the interview, we should go directly to the lab
for a blood sample, and Dr. M. promises to phone Marilyn
tomorrow with the results.

"And one last question, today," I say. "If this immunoglobulin approach doesn't help, are there other options
available?"

"There are several available," Dr. M. replies.

I look over at Marilyn and notice her shaking her head, ever so slightly but I got her message: *Forget it. I'm done with this. I will not undergo any further treatment.*

For several minutes toward the end of our session, Marilyn speaks about why she does not fear death, quoting some passages from my book *Staring at the Sun*, including Nietzsche's phrase to "die at the right time." She speaks of how she has no regrets about how she has lived her life. As I listen, I feel so proud: of her, of her articulateness and her bearing. I have been so extraordinarily fortunate and blessed to have had Marilyn as my life partner. Dr. M., too, is moved by her words, and at the end of our session hugs Marilyn and tells her how beloved she is.

———

For the last few weeks, I'd been aware of dreaming a great deal but, strangely, was unable to recall a single one. But the night following our meeting, I sleep uneasily and clearly recall a fragment of a lengthy, frightening dream. I am holding a large suitcase and hitchhiking on a deserted road. Something unpleasant had preceded this, but I could not recall it. Then a car pulls over and a man beckons me over, wanting to start a conversation about giving me a ride. There is something frightening, almost diabolic about his face: I distrust him and surreptitiously photograph his license plate with my iPhone and email it to an acquaintance. I refuse to get into his car: we stand there in silence for a long while until he ultimately drives off. The last thing I remember is standing alone in the dark on the roadside. No cars pass. I do not know what to do or where to go.

The harder I try to examine the dream, the quicker it fades. But the major thrust of the dream seems clear: I am alone, homeless, frightened, lost in life, and awaiting the end. I tip my hat to the dream maker within.

We do not hear about the lab result on the following day, a Friday, which means waiting until Monday. My agitation unsettles Marilyn who recalls Dr. M. had said she would call us when she received the lab results. I check with my friend David Spiegel, whose recollection is the same as Marilyn's. I'm losing confidence in my ability to listen and recall events.

I grow so impatient that I use my own Stanford faculty ID to check the lab results on my computer, without telling Marilyn. The complexity of the report is daunting, but it appears to me that the results show no significant change and, in despair, I keep this from Marilyn. I sleep poorly again that night, and early the following morning, Marilyn receives an email from Dr. M. telling her that the lab results are cautiously optimistic. She attaches a screen shot that shows a substantial reduction in some of negative indicators over the last few weeks.

Misunderstanding the lab results reminds me, once again, that my MD degree is ancient: I am a medical doctor in name only and entirely unequipped to understand contemporary medical practice or laboratory results. I would never again persuade myself otherwise.

CHAPTER 12

A COMPLETE SURPRISE

I HAVE BEEN ANTICIPATING a visit from Ivory, a friend who has just returned from Copenhagen. Ivory wants to give me some very special chocolates made only in Denmark. I know Ivory through the literary salons for women writers that I hosted for years. She had been one of the members who regularly attended both during the school year and the summer salon when we also included the writers' partners.

It is a treat to bite into the hazelnut chocolates that Ivory opens for Irv and me. I find it so lovely to see this woman again, whom I remember as far back as her pregnancy with her first child, now nine years old. Ivory runs a small publishing house, producing books online and paper editions on demand. (She republished my out-of-print book on women's memoirs of the French Revolution under the title *Compelled to Witness*, which now has had a new life in high school history classes and has even produced some royalties!)

Ivory is telling me about some of her new projects that would help fund her publishing aspirations when the doorbell rings. Before anyone even has the time to go to the front door, it opens and a familiar face appears. Then another. And another. Until about twenty members of my former salon fill the living room! I am *bouche bée*—completely surprised and amazed! How had Ivory arranged this gathering without my having a clue?

It turns out that she had been organizing it for months after I had had to abandon the salons because of my health. This collective visit is a symbolic substitute for the salon I had usually held in our Palo Alto home at the end of summer. But this was not all.

Ivory hands me a beautifully designed book with the title *Letters to Marilyn*. The enormous effort that Ivory has put into producing the book, as well as gathering the salonnières, is obvious. Inside the book are thirty letters written by salonnières, some of whom were unable to be present today. I open it at random and am immediately struck by the importance these women attribute to me as an influence in their lives. One begins: "You may not know how important you've been to me ever since we met!" Another: "What worlds you have opened up to me!" And another: "I have been so privileged and lucky to know you!"

How can one react honestly and gracefully to such testimonials? I am overwhelmed. But alongside the sense of gratitude, I also feel, deep inside, that I do not deserve such an outpouring of praise. Over the past months, so many people have already sent me expressions of praise and concern by way of letters and flowers and food. Yet this group is special—a group of writers, professors, independent scholars, photographers, and filmmakers, who have been in my life for over half a century. Stina Katchadourian, whom I have known since 1966, begins her letter: "Friend, confidant, mentor, wise woman, pencil-in-hand woman, always-there woman, rock, almost-relative, sister." This and so many of the other letters make me cry, and I save them all to read, over and over again.

Letters to Marilyn is a "limited edition of one copy," edited by Ivory Madison and designed by Ashley Ingram. The cover shows a photo of me, taken some thirty-five years ago, sitting before my desk. There never has been, in my biased opinion, a more beautiful limited-edition book. Nor a more meaningful one for a person nearing the end of her life.

An hour passes quickly, and I speak to each person individually. It is especially meaningful to sit with Barbara Babcock, Stanford professor of law, who has been undergoing chemo treatment for breast cancer. She has been one of my first models in bravery. Long before I was diagnosed with multiple myeloma, we used to meet regularly at restaurants or at her house when she was sick. Since beginning my own treatments, however, we had not seen each other. We speak about the miseries associated with our conditions and also about the loving support of our husbands.

I am so glad to see Myra Strober, always a dear friend and colleague since she hired me as a senior researcher and administrator at the old CROW (Center for Research on Women) in 1976. Without Myra, the second half of my life would have been entirely different. And I feel such gratitude that she could come today despite her own recent hip surgery several weeks earlier and her husband's severe Parkinson's disease.

These two women, Barbara and Myra, have the distinction of being the first women hired by the Stanford Law School (Barbara) and the Stanford Business School (Myra) in 1972. Each has mentored many other women in their long careers, and each has written an autobiography of their personal and professional experiences.

Also among the familiar faces is Meg Clayton. I ask her to tell us about her new historical novel, *The Last Train to London*, to be published shortly in English and with contracts for nineteen translations! I've had the privilege of observing Meg's transformation over the last few years into a truly significant writer. In her letter to me, Meg quotes "Let Evening Come" by Jane Kenyon that the late John Felstiner had read aloud years ago in this very living room where we were now sitting. That poem, excerpted in part here, is now so appropriate to my life situation:

> Let the fox go back to its sandy den.
> Let the wind die down. Let the shed
> go black inside. Let evening come.
> To the bottle in the ditch, to the scoop
> in the oats, to air in the lung
> let evening come.
> Let it come, as it will and don't
> be afraid. God does not leave us
> comfortless, so let evening come.

After everyone has gone, I sit for a long time thinking about the outpouring of love today. Could I really have been as kind and generous as my friends said I was? If that were true, I inherited much of my character from my mother, the sweetest, kindest person I ever knew. My mom was kind to everyone. Even into her eighties, she would ring at the door of her fellow apartment dwellers and ask if she could bring something back from the store for them. Later, when we placed her in a nursing home near us in Palo Alto, she always kept sweets to give to the grandchildren when they came to visit. She brought me up to be naturally sociable and to be "a giver rather than a taker." My mother taught me to ask myself, beforehand, how my words and actions would make another person feel. Of course, I did not always follow her example. There are times I remember having been thoughtlessly, and even intentionally, selfish at the expense of another person. Fortunately, my friends today have seen only my better side.

Yet there is a somewhat darker train of thought that keeps bumping into this Pollyanna picture of myself: surely much of this praise is inspired by my illness and the thought that I won't be here much longer. Perhaps this will be the last time I see many of these people. Were they here to "pay their last respects"? Well, even if that is true, I'll take it. It was a lovely day, one of a kind that I shall treasure for the rest of my life, however long or short that may be.

CHAPTER 13

SO NOW YOU KNOW

SINCE OUR LAST MEETING with Dr. M., who told us that there were, finally, some lab findings suggesting Marilyn is improving, our life has undergone a major change. Marilyn has returned to me. She is not going to die in the near future—and today I suspect she will probably outlive me. I've got my old Marilyn back again, and we've had some wonderful days.

As usual, I go with her to the hospital for several hours on Wednesday when she gets her infusion. For a day or two, she is more perky, more like herself. Usually she feels good on Thursdays, but this week is different: she is in exceptionally good humor. She is the Marilyn I knew before she got sick, the Marilyn I haven't seen for a long time.

On Friday, two days after her chemotherapy infusion, she still feels good enough to go to a restaurant for dinner. This is perhaps only the third time since her illness began, several months ago, that we've dined out. We choose our usual dependable restaurant, Fuki Sushi, just a few blocks from our home. There are reliable dishes there, such as zosui and miso soup, that Marilyn can digest easily. We've dined there perhaps five hundred times over the past fifty years. One year they presented us with a set of steak knives for being their most loyal customers.

The following morning, Saturday, Marilyn awakes with a big smile on her face. "I've had a vivid dream—the funniest dream in months, perhaps years.

"I'm at my childhood home in Washington, DC, and I have snuck up the stairs to my bedroom with a man whose face I couldn't see. He gets into bed with me, and we start to make love but instead he pees in the bed. I have to get up and change the sheets. Then I go downstairs to make a cup of tea, and as I'm coming back up the steps I hear some noise or movement across the hall in my mother's room. I knock at the door and open it a trifle. Who do I see there but our son Ben, naked and sitting in my mother's bed, with a big smirk on his face?

"My mother looks at me and says, 'So, now you know!'

"I answer, 'There's also somebody in my bedroom. Now you know.'"

We both laugh at this absurd dream and try unsuccessfully to make sense of it. Marilyn dreams of being young in the home where she grew up. But she has an affair with an unknown man, an incontinent man who pees in the bed, the act of an old man. And then the odd hilarious meeting with her mother, a very sweet, loving woman who is in bed with our adult son Ben.

Incest, time travel, absurd humor, life stages, and a rebellion against aging—it's all there!

Later that day Marilyn tells me she thought the dream had been triggered by seeing Ben sitting in bed with me while we were having a conversation. It was the same smile on his face that she saw in the dream. Naturally, we turn to Freud's Oedipal interpretation of mother-son incest, which Marilyn had disguised by attributing it to her mother. As for the older lover, it was probably me, even though I have yet to pee in bed.

Marilyn is in such high spirits for the entire day that I feel my mind recalibrating: I have my Marilyn back again! But, alas, not for long: by the following afternoon, she is again nauseated and so fatigued she can hardly lift herself from the couch. Her sudden reversal from just the day before is incomprehensible, and I feel helpless again. I tell her, and mean it, that I so wish I could take her disease and be nauseated and fatigued for her.

These huge fluctuations persist. The next day, she once again feels herself, and all in all, she seems to be improving. Marilyn's illness has overshadowed all else, but now I have time to consider the course of my own life. I have very few peers—all my closest and oldest friends and acquaintances have died. Aside from Marilyn only a couple of friends from the deep past still live and breathe. There is my cousin, Jay, three years younger, whom I've known since he was born. He lives in Washington, DC, and we speak by phone at least four or five times a week. But neither of us is up to traveling, and it's unlikely I'll ever again see him again in the flesh. I speak weekly on the phone with Saul Spiro, who was a resident with me at Johns Hopkins. He lives in Washington state but is too ill to travel. Just yesterday I had read in the *Stanford Report* that Stanley Schrier had died. A friend and neighbor from long ago, Stanley was the Stanford hematology professor who referred us to Dr. M. In his obituary, I learn he was 90, two years older than I. Two more years—that seems about right: I will probably live two more years. But, if Marilyn weren't there, I wouldn't want to stay around that long.

I am now a retired man and have given up the work I love. I sorely miss my therapy practice. It's only been a few months since retiring as a therapist, and I still see three or four patients weekly for a single consultation. But my life's work as a therapist has ended, and I'm in mourning for it. I miss the deep intimacy of the therapy process. No one now, except Marilyn, invites me into the deepest and darkest chambers of herself.

As I contemplate how best to describe the depth and extent of my loss, a patient's face comes to mind. How strange that this particular person appears in my mind: I saw her only once a great many years ago. But just a couple of weeks ago, as I was browsing through some of my old unpublished writings, I came across these pages of a story that I had begun to write about her.

On the day of my sixty-fifth birthday, Phyllis, a somber, attractive, elderly woman entered my office. Obviously highly uncomfortable, she sat birdlike perched on the very edge of her chair as though prepared to take flight at any moment.

"Welcome, Phyllis. I'm Irv Yalom, and I know from your email only that your sleep is poor and that you're often anxious. Shall we start right in? Tell me more about it."

But Phyllis was too ill at ease to start right in. "I need a minute or two—I don't often talk about myself, my hidden self." She scanned my office, and her eyes fixated upon an autographed photograph of the great New York Yankee baseball player Joe DiMaggio hanging on the wall.

"He was one of my childhood heroes," I commented.

Phyllis broke out into a big smile. "Joe DiMaggio—I know him—that is, know about him. I grew up in San Francisco in North Beach, not far from where he lived and only a couple of blocks from the church where he and Marilyn Monroe were married."

"Yes, I spent a lot of time in North Beach too, often had lunch at DiMaggio's restaurant—I think it was Dominic's, his brother's, restaurant. Today it's turned into "Original Joe's." You ever see him play?"

"Only on TV. I loved to watch him run the bases. So much grace. I saw him a couple of times walking around the Marina area. That's where he lives now."

Noticing that she had slowly settled back into her chair, making herself more comfortable, I thought it was time to get down to business. "So tell me about yourself, Phyllis, and tell me what brings you here to see me today."

"Well, I'm 83 and worked most of my life as a nurse anesthetist. Retired several years ago. I live alone. Never married. Pretty isolated, I'm sure you'd think. No family, except a distant half-brother, and I suffer a lot from insomnia and anxiety." Her lips quivered as she smiled at me. She seemed almost apologetic for making me work hard.

"I see that it's not easy talking openly about yourself, Phyllis. I'm guessing that this is the first time you've spoken to a therapist?"

She nodded.

"Tell me, why now? What helped you make this decision to call me now?"

"No sudden event. Things are just continuing to get worse, especially the insomnia and isolation."

"And why me?"

"I've read a lot of your books. Just felt I could trust you. Most recently *Lying on the Couch*. You seemed flexible, and kind, and not practicing in a strait jacket. Most importantly, I don't see you as judgmental."

It was clear she was dealing with a lot of guilt. I kept my voice soft: "You're right. I don't feel judgmental. I'm on your side. I'm here to help you."

Phyllis dived in and began describing her traumatic youth. Her father disappeared when she was three. She never heard from him again nor would her mother ever again mention his name. Her mother, she said, was a vicious, cold, narcissistic woman, and when one of the many men her mother brought home attempted to abuse her, Phyllis ran away from home at 15, prostituted herself, lived with a series of men, and then, miraculously, managed to put herself through high school, college, and nursing school. She had worked her entire adult life as a nurse anesthetist.

She sat back in her chair, took a couple of deep breaths, and continued, "So, in a nutshell, that's my life. Now for the hard part. Some years ago my sister contacted me to tell me that our mother was in the late stages of lung cancer; she was on oxygen and was now comatose in a hospice unit. 'She's near death,' I remember my sister saying, 'and I've been with her the last three nights and am at the end of my string. Please, Phyllis, could you come and spend tonight with her? She's not conscious—you won't need to talk to her.'

"I agreed—my sister and I had reconnected some years before and even begun having lunch every month or two. I agreed to her request but did it for my sister, not my mother. I hadn't seen my mother for many decades and, as I've told you, I didn't give a rat's ass about her and I agreed to sit with her that night only to give my sister some rest. At about three in the morning—I remember it so clearly, like it was yesterday—my mother's breathing grew irregular and stertorous and the foam of pulmonary edema formed on her lips. I've been through this with so many patients and I knew her last breath was coming. I was certain it was coming any minute."

Phyllis's head was bowed. She paused for several seconds and then, looking up at me, she whispered, "I've got to tell someone—can I trust you?"

I nodded.

"I turned off the oxygen . . . turned it off just before the last breath."

We sat in silence for a while. Then she said. "Was it pity or revenge? I keep asking myself."

"Or maybe a tad of both," I said. "Or maybe it's time to let the question go. How awful this must have been for you to hold this all to yourself for so many years. What's it like for you to finally share this?"

"It's too scary to even discuss that."

"Try to stay with it. I appreciate that you've trusted me with this scalding secret. What would help? Is there something you can ask me, something I could say, that might release you or help you in some fashion?"

"I need to tell you that I'm not a murderer. I've sat through last moments with many patients. So many patients. She had only one more breath. Two at the most."

"Let me tell you what I'm thinking . . ."

Phyllis's eyes shot up to mine—as though her life depended on my next words.

"I'm thinking of that little girl, that helpless, abused, powerless girl, that young girl so subject to fate, and the demands and whims of others. How tragic that you had to be the one to witness your mother's last moments. And how understandable that you had to claim power."

Though there were twenty minutes left in our hour. Phyllis gathered up her belongings, stood, put her check on the table, mouthed "thank you," and left. I never saw or heard from her again.

———

That encounter so many years ago conveys what I will miss for the rest of my life: the sense of engagement, of being trusted, of sharing deep and dark moments with another. And, most of all, the opportunity to offer so much to another person. That's been my way of life for so many years. I treasure it. I will miss it. Such a contrast with a passive life in which I am assisted by a caretaker—a life that I fear lies not too far ahead.

Marilyn asks me why I have chosen this story rather than any others from my copious notes. I give the same answer— that it represents the intimate encounters I will no longer have with my patients. She suggests that it may have something to do with end of life issues, the moment when one finally pulls the plug. Perhaps she is right.

CHAPTER 14

DEATH SENTENCE

DR. M. CALLED YESTERDAY to tell me that I should not continue with the immunoglobulin therapy. The latest lab results indicate it is not working, and in an odd way, I feel relieved. I will not have to experience the toxic aftereffects from the drugs that have been administered since early this year. This week they were worse than usual, and I kept asking myself, "Is it worth prolonging life at such a cost?"

Of course, I don't know what pain is in store for me by just letting the disease run its course. The people in palliative medicine assure me that they will do everything possible to alleviate the suffering, but I don't even want to begin to imagine what that will be like. For now, it is quite enough to contemplate death.

Death at the age of 87 is no tragedy, especially when I think of all the younger people who have died. This week, the reporter Cokie Roberts died at 75. I felt a special kinship with her as a co-recipient of a Wellesley Distinguished

Alumnae award. My portrait hangs in a stately hall at the college along with hers and those of many more famous alums, such as Hillary Clinton and Madeleine Albright. It gives me a sense of pride to think that I, too, was part of the feminist movement that advanced women's rights during the last two generations. That was my time. What will happen in the future after my death is no longer in my hands.

I guess I have been thinking about death for so long that it comes as no surprise to me. By now, my children have all been informed, and I am sustained by their love. My son Reid and his wife, Loredana, took care of us for the weekend, making a large supply of chicken soup and apple compote for me. Eve rushed over from Berkeley and helped us digest the bad news. Victor will spend tomorrow night with us, and Ben will arrive later this week.

If I am up to it, I shall go with Irv and Eve to Ben's new production in San Francisco—*Dionysus Was Such a Nice Man*. Somehow Ben has managed to keep his theater company together into its twenty-first season. It got a terrific review in the *San Francisco Chronicle* and I am so happy for him; I really would like to see his play, but it depends on my strength and condition. That's my new formula: focus on yourself and your daily needs. It's time to let the rest of the world take care of itself.

Of course, I do worry about Irv. For months now he has been taking care of me, and I fear he will just wear himself out. With his own health issues on top of mine, he needs all the help he can get. Our friend Mary, who took care of her husband for over three years before he died, has talked to me about the plight of caretakers. She was able to join a group of caretakers with similar problems, and together they shared their burdens with each other. Even now, two years after her husband's death, she meets regularly with these women.

It is unlikely that Irv would ever use such a support system, not to mention the fact that, in Mary's case, all the caretakers were women. For a great many years, Irv has met every week with a group of psychiatrists to discuss their personal problems, and I believe this is helpful for him. Although he knows rationally that I am dying, he still maintains some form of denial. When I wondered out loud if I would still be here at Christmas, he looked at me incredulously—of course I would preside over the family gathering as always. I do not know if it is better to talk about the short time ahead of me or to leave him in denial.

———

The idea of death does not frighten me. I do not believe in an afterlife beyond a "reintegration into the cosmos," and I can accept the idea that I shall no longer exist. My body will ultimately disintegrate into the earth. When my mother died over twenty years ago, she was buried in the Alta Mesa cemetery within walking distance of our house. At that time, we also bought two cemetery plots near hers for ourselves. Frequent visits to that cemetery initiated *The American Resting Place* book project with my son Reid and opened up a whole new perspective on burial and cremation.

Today, cremation is more popular in America than traditional burial, and ecological concerns are coming more and more to the fore. For example, in Washington state one can be buried in in such a way as to turn one's body into compost. In California, a startup company is buying up forest and allowing individuals to fertilize a specific tree. I like the idea of being buried in a simple wooden coffin within walking distance of our home, right across from the high school that our four children attended. In the future, if they come to visit my grave, they will be surrounded by childhood memories.

As I feel my life coming to an end, how shall I take leave of my friends? So many people have been kind to me during my illness, and I do not want to disappear from their lives without letting them know how much they have meant to me. A phone call to say goodbye takes a great deal of energy. A letter feels more substantial, but will I have the time and the stamina to write each one? In a certain Jewish tradition, according to Elana Zaiman in her book *The Forever Letter*, one writes a last letter to loved ones to communicate one's feelings toward that person and any salient bits of wisdom one wishes to convey. Whatever wisdom I have acquired during my lifetime is not something I can now put into a short letter. I hope I can at least live up to my expectations of dying in such a way as to cause as little pain to others . . . and to myself.

My way of saying farewell to my friends will probably be centered around a late afternoon cup of tea. I have already begun to see a few of my close friends for this purpose and will schedule others in the weeks to come. I hope there will be time to say goodbye in person to everyone who has enriched my life and sustained me in these last difficult months.

It's weird to realize that if I want to do anything, I'll have to do it quickly. It occurs to me that I should designate a container for each child and fill it with items that might be of interest to them or their children or grandchildren in the future. I imagine this box stuck away in someone's attic and then examined by a distant offspring when Irv and I are only names on their genealogical chart. What will they make of an item identified as "Irv's high school fraternity pin, given to Marilyn in 1948"? Will they be delighted by an album of photos taken at our fiftieth wedding anniversary? Should I include a scrapbook of reviews of my book *A History of the Breast* published in 1997?

It is so hard to realize that all the books and papers and objects that have accompanied my life will have little meaning for my children and grandchildren. In fact, they will probably be a burden for them. I know I shall be doing them a service by getting rid of as much "stuff" as possible.

———

When Irv and I visit Dr. M. for the last time, I pose two questions to her: How much longer can I expect to live and how do we initiate assisted suicide?

Her response to the first question is, "One can't be certain, of course, but my guess would be in the neighborhood of two months."

This comes as a shock. I was expecting a somewhat longer period. This will barely give me time to see all my close friends once more and to follow up on the idea of a container of meaningful objects for each child.

Fortunately, we have already scheduled a "celebration" in just two weeks for all the children and their offspring. The cause of the celebration was initially our son Victor's sixtieth birthday, as well as three other family members with October birthdays—our sons' three wives, Marie-Helene, Anisa, and Loredana. Now I am labeling this event "Four Birthdays and a Funeral" in a parody of a film with a similar name. It helps to keep a sense of humor.

As for assisted suicide, that requires sign-off by two physicians, the criteria being that the patient is near death with no possible cure in sight. I believe Dr. M. from hematology and Dr. S. from palliative medicine will sign off for me in my last weeks of life. I am surprised to learn that death will be caused by swallowing a large number of pills, not by injection or even a single pill.

Well, so far, I am relatively calm. After ten months of feeling awful most of the time, it's a relief to know that my misery will come to an end. In an odd way, I feel that I have "paid" for any sins or wrongdoings I have committed during my lifetime. The religious concept of judgment and punishment or reward after death has worked its way into my sense of a secular equivalent: I feel I have already suffered enough physically before I die. And who knows what is yet in store for me, before I kiss Irv for the last time?

CHAPTER 15

FAREWELL TO CHEMOTHERAPY— AND TO HOPE

I'VE FEARED THE DAY when we would meet with Dr. M. for an in-depth discussion of ending treatment. Dr. M. arrives promptly to our appointment and answers all of our many questions in a knowledgeable and kind fashion. I inquire about why Marilyn had failed to respond to treatment: we had known or heard about so many acquaintances who lived for years, for decades with multiple myeloma. She responds with a sad look on her face that medical science doesn't know why some patients with this disease fail to respond to treatment or why some, like Marilyn, experience such toxic side effects that make therapy impossible.

Then Marilyn, never shy, cuts to the chase and asks, "How much time do I have? How long do you think I'll live?"

I am shocked—and feel sorry for Dr. M. I would hate to be in her shoes. But she seems unfazed and gives a straight answer, "No one can be exact about an answer, but I would estimate that it might be in the neighborhood of one to two months."

I gasp at this. We both do: we had hoped for and expected three to six more months. Strange how anxiety disrupts perception. I am in such shock that my mind shifts gears, and I begin to wonder how often Dr. M. has to engage in such discussions. I look at her: she is an attractive, soft spoken, compassionate person. I hope she has someone to talk to about the stress she must experience on a daily basis. I marvel at my mind's agility, caught it in the act of protecting myself: no sooner have I heard the words "one to two months" then I suddenly switch my focus elsewhere and begin thinking of Dr. M.'s daily experience. My mind whirls from one place to another: I cannot bear to hold the thought that my Marilyn might not live more than a month.

Marilyn, remarkable as ever, seems unfazed. She'd like to discuss physician-assisted suicide, and then asks Dr. M. if she would agree be one of those two physicians required to sign approval. I enter a state of shock. I'm not thinking coherently. I'm troubled by learning that she would die by swallowing pills. I had always thought it would be via an IV injection. Whereas I can throw several pills in my mouth and swallow them easily, Marilyn can only swallow one pill at a time deliberately and slowly. What will happen when the time comes? I imagine I could use a mortar and pestle and grind the pills and make an emulsion of the powder. Then I start to imagine her lifting the emulsion to her lips, but that is too much to ask of myself and the images just blur away.

I begin to weep. I think of how I've always taken care of Marilyn—she was just under five feet tall and weighed barely a hundred pounds when I first met her seventy-four years ago. I suddenly imagine a scene of my handing her lethal pills and seeing her gagging on them, one after the other. I sweep this horrific scene from my mind, which immediately replaces them with images of Marilyn giving a valedictorian address both at McFarland, our junior high school, and at Roosevelt, our high school. I was bigger and stronger and knew about the world of science and always, always, tried to take care of Marilyn, always tried to keep her safe. And yet, now, I shudder as I imagine holding those killing pills and handing them to her one by one.

The following morning I awake at 5 A.M. with a blazing insight. "Don't you realize," I said to myself, "dying is not in the future: Marilyn is *already* dying." She eats very little and seems terminally fatigued. I can't even get her to walk five minutes to the mailbox at the end of our driveway. She is dying *now*—it's not something that will come to pass. *It's happening now.* We are in the midst of it. Sometimes I imagine my taking the pills and dying together with her. I imagine my therapist friends discussing among themselves whether they should admit me to the inpatient psychiatry ward because I am a suicide risk.

CHAPTER 16

FROM PALLIATIVE CARE TO HOSPICE

HAVING NOTHING MORE to offer, Dr. M. refers Marilyn to palliative care, the branch of medicine which focuses entirely on reducing pain and making patients as comfortable as possible. Marilyn and I, accompanied by our daughter, Eve, have a long session with Dr. S., the chief of palliative care, a warm and gracious woman who takes a complete medical history, conducts a physical exam, and prescribes medications for Marilyn's symptoms—her ongoing nausea, disturbing skin lesions, and extreme fatigue.

Marilyn patiently answers all her inquiries but soon turns to the topic paramount in her mind: physician-assisted suicide. Dr. S. answers all of Marilyn's questions in a gentle and caring fashion but makes clear that she does not favor this step. She emphasizes that her work is to make sure that her patients do not suffer and to allow them to die comfortably and painlessly from their illness.

Moreover, Dr. S. informs us that physician-assisted suicide is a complex step requiring considerable administrative paperwork. She informs us that the mode of death, ingestion of lethal pills, has to be self-administered: the physician is not permitted to assist the patient to ingest these pills. When I comment that Marilyn has considerable problems swallowing pills, Dr. S. mentions that it might be possible to grind the pills to powder and mix them with a drink. She acknowledges she has very little experience, having participated in only one physician-assisted death.

Marilyn, however, persists and asks Dr. S. if she would agree to be one of the two required physicians who would sign the order. Dr. S. inhales deeply, hesitates, then agrees but repeats that she hopes this will not be necessary. She then raises the issue of referring Marilyn to a hospice. She explains that the hospice staff would regularly visit our home and make sure that Marilyn is without pain and as comfortable as possible. She will contact two nearby hospices, who would each send a member of their staff to inform us about what their hospice could offer, and we can select one of the two.

Both of the hospice representatives who visit us at home are well informed and kind. How to choose between them? Marilyn learns that a close friend's husband had recently had excellent hospice care by Mission Hospice, so we chose to work with Mission. Very soon thereafter we are visited by the hospice nurse and social worker and two days later by Dr. P., the hospice physician. He spends an hour and a half with us. We were both impressed and soothed by him. I regard him as one of the most caring, empathic physicians I've ever encountered and silently hope he will be available to take care of me when it is my time to die.

About fifteen minutes into our discussion with Dr. P., Marilyn can't hold back and again raises the question of doctor-assisted suicide. Dr. P.'s answer is astonishingly different from any that we had previously encountered: he is highly sympathetic to the idea, though he prefers the term "physician-attended dying." He reassures Marilyn that he personally would facilitate her dying when the appropriate time comes. He assures her that if she makes that choice, he would remain with her and would prepare an emulsion of the pills that she could sip through a straw and easily swallow. He tells us that he has participated in over a hundred such deaths, and he agrees wholeheartedly with this choice whenever the patient is in much pain, with no hope of recovery.

Those words have a powerfully calming effect for Marilyn—for both of us—yet, at the same time, it makes her death more real. *Marilyn is going to die soon. Marilyn is going to die soon. Marilyn is going to die soon.* That thought is too much for me, and I continue to shove it from my mind. Denial reigns. I turn my eyes away. I don't, won't, look this straight in the face.

———

A few days later, two of our children sleep over, our oldest, our daughter, Eve, and our youngest, Ben. I wake up early, walk down to my office, and spend two hours going over the editor's proofs of a chapter in the new edition of my group therapy textbook. About 10:30, I come up to the house where Marilyn is sitting at the table finishing her breakfast, sipping her tea, and reading the morning newspaper.

"Where are the kids?" I ask. Kids indeed! My daughter is 64, and my son is 50. (My two other sons are 62 and 59.)

"Oh," Marilyn says in a calm, matter-of-fact tone, "they're at the undertakers, making arrangements for the funeral, and then they'll be visiting the cemetery, checking out our burial sites. We'll be right next to my mother."

To my own surprise, I burst out crying and my tears flow for several minutes. Marilyn hugs me while I try to regain control of myself. Between sobs, I say, "How can you speak so lightly about this? I cannot bear the thought of your dying. I cannot cope with the thought of living in a world without you."

She pulls me toward her and says, "Irv, don't forget I've been living in pain and misery for ten months now. I've said to you again and again *that I cannot bear the thought of living like this any longer.* I welcome death, I welcome being free of pain and nausea and this chemo brain and this continual fatigue and this feeling awful. Please understand me: trust me—I'm certain that if you had lived all these months in my condition you'd feel the same way. I'm alive now only because of you. I'm devastated at the thought of leaving you. But, Irv, it's time. Please, you've got to let me go."

This is not the first time I have heard these words. But perhaps it is the first time I let them penetrate my mind. Perhaps for the very first time, I truly grasp that if I had gone through the last ten months of what Marilyn has experienced, I would be feeling precisely the same way! If I had lived with that much anguish, I'd be welcoming death, just like Marilyn.

For a moment, just for a moment, I feel some of my old physician-words clustering together struggling to become a rebuttal: You don't have to suffer pain. We've got morphine for your pain, we've got steroids for your fatigue, we've got . . . we've got . . . But I couldn't give voice to such inauthentic words.

We just hold each other, both of us weeping. For the first time Marilyn talks about my life after her death. "Irv, it won't be so bad. The kids will always be visiting. Your friends will be dropping in all the time. If you're too much alone in this big house, you can always ask Gloria, our housekeeper, and her husband to move rent-free into my office and always be available if you needed them."

I interrupt her: I had vowed to myself I would never impose the burden upon Marilyn of worrying about my life without her. I hug her and tell her for the thousandth time how much I love her and admire her and owe every particle of my success in life to her.

As always, she demurs and speaks of my talent, my creation of so many varied worlds in my writing. "You had it in you. Your own creativity. I just helped you uncork it."

"My success came from my brain, my imagination—yes, I know that, my darling. But I also know that you opened the window of the creative world for me. If not for you, I would have done exactly what all my close buddies in medical school did: I would have gone into practice in Washington, DC. Though that would have been a good life, not a single one of my books would have ever seen the light of day. You introduced me to higher forms of literature—remember I rushed through college in only three years taking a premed science curriculum. You were my only link with the classics, with great literature, with philosophy: you broadened my narrow view of the world. You introduced me to the great writers and thinkers."

———

That evening our close friends Denny and Josie visit, bringing a homemade dinner. Denny is a colleague, one of the best psychotherapists I've ever known and also a jazz pianist of national repute. When Denny and I take a stroll alone, I lay out what I'm facing. He knows well the overwhelming importance Marilyn is in my life (as is his wife to him). I knew he would agree with Marilyn's decision to have physician-assisted suicide: he had often voiced his support of anyone's right to end one's life when the pain is unbearable and without hope for recovery.

I tell him that this is a horrific time of life for me, that Marilyn is off all treatment for multiple myeloma, but someday soon it will inevitably make its reappearance. That, day by day, I wait fearfully. That I'll never forget the original onset when Marilyn awakened me, screaming with back pain from a fractured vertebrae caused by the myeloma.

Denny is unusually quiet: generally he is extremely responsive and articulate, one of the most expressive and intelligent men that I know. His silence frightens me: I fear I laid too much on him.

The following morning when Marilyn and I are at breakfast she mentions, in passing, that she felt some pain in her back. I gasp silently: I thought, of course, of her fractured vertebrae and her terrible pain—her first symptom of multiple myeloma. I feel terror arising: I have been dreading the reappearance of her multiple myeloma. Were my worst fears coming to pass? I haven't done physical examinations for scores of years, but I could have easily put my hands on her back and applied a little pressure on each of her vertebrae and identified the location of the pain. But I could not bring myself to do this. No loving husband should be in this position. Besides, my daughter, also an MD, would be arriving shortly, and I could ask her to examine her mother's back. How horrible to think there might be no relief from her pain aside from morphine . . . and death.

I begin to berate myself. After all, I have worked with so many bereaved individuals, and the great majority of them suffered the same loss that I am facing now. Yes, without doubt: I am experiencing my suffering as worse than theirs by repeatedly emphasizing the uniqueness of my loss—how long and how much I have loved my wife.

I have worked with so many bereaved spouses who eventually improved—I know it is slow, between one to two years—but it will happen. And yet I sabotage my efforts to comfort myself by immediately focusing on my many burdens—my age, my memory problems, my physical problems, especially my balance problems which make it difficult to walk without a cane or walker. But, I have a quick rejoinder to this dark self: Irv, Good Lord—look at your advantages: your knowledge of the mind and how much you know about overcoming painful moments. And, Irv, you have a great many supports—four loving devoted children and eight grandchildren none of whom would refuse any request from you. And think of the large number of friends who surround you. You have the financial means and the ability to stay in your beautiful home or enter any residential community. And, Irv, most importantly, you, too, like Marilyn, have no regrets—you've lived a long and gratifying life—you've had far more success than you would have ever imagined—you've helped so many patients, sold millions of copies of your books in thirty languages, and receive reams of fan mail every day.

So, I tell myself, it is time to stop whining. Why are you exaggerating your despair, Irv—is it a plea for help? Are you still trying to show Marilyn how much you love her? By God she knows that by now. And the depth of your sadness only makes her feel worse. Yes, yes, I respond. I know she does not want me to sink into terminal despair—she wants me to be happy and to prosper—she does not want me to die with her. I do not have to keep on displaying my pain. Time to give myself a kick in the ass.

There is an endless procession of friends and acquaintances wishing to see Marilyn, and I take the responsibility of protecting her from exhausting herself amidst the sheer numbers of loving visitors. I act as timekeeper and, as courteously as possible, limit visits to thirty minutes. My daughter has set up a website that will allow Marilyn's friends to receive news about her condition.

Marilyn soldiers on. When friends join us for dinner, I admire how she keeps the conversation going, asking questions about people's lives and helping everyone enjoy themselves. It's true I have skills for talking and working with my students and patients, but her general social skills are unparalleled. One or more of our four children often visit and spend the night. I always enjoy their presence, and invariably there will animated discussion, often chess games, and sometimes pinochle.

But however much I love our children, I greatly treasure my evenings alone with Marilyn. For several months, I have had total responsibility for meals: Marilyn's stomach is extremely sensitive, and she eats the same simple food every day—chicken broth with rice and carrots. I fix some simple dinner for myself or occasionally order a take-out dinner from a restaurant. Then the TV news, and Marilyn's prayer that Trump be impeached while she is alive to witness it. Often we search for a film—not an easy task because Marilyn's memory is too good and, almost always, she prefers a new film—and watch half of the film one night and the other half the next day.

Tonight after dinner, we enjoy watching the old film *Arsenic and Old Lace* with Cary Grant and Raymond Massey. We hold hands. I can't stop touching her. Enjoying the film, I gaze at Marilyn in amazement as I think how little time is left for us. I know . . . we know . . . that she is going to die fairly soon, probably most likely within the next four weeks. It seems surreal. We're simply waiting for the multiple myeloma to wreak havoc on her smile and her beautiful body. I am frightened for her, and I'm amazed at her disposition and her courage. Not once have I heard her say she's frightened or dismayed by her bad luck of being visited by this disease.

I am extremely aware of my own deterioration. Too often I am confused about my schedule and often look at the wrong page of my schedule book. I thought a patient was coming at three today and she came at four. I thought we would be meeting on Zoom and she arrived in person. I feel I am beginning to lose it. I feel incapable. With one exception: when I actually start a consultation with a patient, I feel my old self and almost without exception I sense I've given each patient I've seen, even in a single session, something valuable.

It appears to me that my balance, my ability to walk, and my memory are all rapidly deteriorating. And now for the very first time, I'm beginning to wonder if I really can live in this house by myself after Marilyn dies. What a pity we can't die together. Where and how I shall live has, I've recently learned, been a topic of considerable conversation among my children. The other day my daughter, Eve, said she was looking into changing the stove and burners from gas to electric because she feared I'd accidentally leave the burners on and burn down the house. I was annoyed by her treating me like a child and making decisions about my kitchen, yet there is a part of me that agrees with her. When she and all my other children opine that I can't stay here alone in the house, I'm annoyed and I bristle—but not too much because I fear they're right. It's not the loneliness that's the issue—it's the safety.

I haven't looked deeply at my future nor seriously considered hiring someone to live with me. I think I refrain from spending much time thinking about it because I consider it a betrayal to Marilyn. I've talked about it the last couple of days with friends, all of whom support my inclination to stay in the home I love so much. I've lived and worked in the same community for a great many decades, and I'm surrounded with family and friends and, for the time being, I'm determined to stay in my home. I imagine that between my friends and children, I'd have company three evenings a week and be perfectly comfortable being alone the rest of the time.

Basically I'm not a highly social person—my wife has always filled that role in the family. I remember my first meeting with Marilyn: I was a teenager, gambling in the bowling alley (I did have a penchant for gambling—still have remnants of it). Someone, not a close friend and a fairly disreputable guy, suggested that we go to a party at Marilyn Koenick's home. It was so crowded that the only way we could enter was through the window. In the midst of a packed house, there was Marilyn, holding court. I took one look at her and made my way through the crowd to introduce myself to her. This was a highly unusual act on my part: never before or after have I been so socially bold. But it was indeed love at first sight! I phoned her the very next night—my first phone call to a girl.

As I think about life without Marilyn, grief and anxiety flares. My mind is acting primitively: it's as if thinking about my future without Marilyn is a betrayal—a traitorous act that might hasten her death. "Traitorous" feels like the correct term: when I make plans for my life after Marilyn's death, it feels like treason. I should be entirely consumed with her, about our past, about how we spend our time now with one another, about our all too brief future.

A sudden inspiration! I ask myself to imagine how it would be if things were reversed. Suppose it were I who was dying, and Marilyn who was taking loving care of me as she has always done? Suppose I knew I had only a few weeks to live. Would I be concerned about how Marilyn would fare without me? Absolutely! I'd be very much concerned about her and wish nothing but the very best life for her. An instantly therapeutic thought. I already feel much better.

CHAPTER 17

HOSPICE CARE

HOSPICE. That's a word I've always associated with the last gasps of a dying patient. And, yet, here I am making appointments with the hospice team. I'm still walking about. Still taking baths on my own. Still reading and writing. Still having lucid conversations with visitors. Despite ongoing fatigue, I am still functional.

A visit from Dr. P., the Mission Hospice physician, is very reassuring. He is exceptionally easy to talk to, knowledgeable and empathic. He has had long experience caring for patients at the end of life, seeing to it that their pain is relieved as much as possible through a variety of medication and other forms of treatment, including meditation and massage. If I don't have unbearable pain, I think I can soldier on to the end with a modicum of dignity. Moreover, I have great confidence in him: he has personally assisted the death of about one hundred patients and assured me he would take care of everything. I feel very comfortable and assured by putting myself into his hands.

We also meet with the nurse and social worker who will be following my case. From now on, the nurse will come once a week to check me out and see how my disease is progressing. She, too, is very knowledgeable and empathic, and I feel reassured by the thought of her weekly visits. I even receive a phone call from a volunteer member of the hospice team offering to come to the house and give me a massage. Since I do love massages, I immediately say yes and set up an appointment. I'm curious to meet someone who volunteers gratis for hospice care. It's almost an embarrassment to have so much attention lavished on this 87-year-old dying body, when so many other people get no care at all.

People, including Irv, keep admiring my ability to remain calm. Yes, on the whole, I do feel calm. Only occasionally, in dreams, does my anguish break through. But on the whole, I have come to accept the fact that I shall soon be dead. The sadness—the great sadness of saying goodbye to family and friends—does not seem to alter my ability to perform the simple acts of living day to day with reasonably good cheer. This is not a veneer: after nine months of toxic treatments and feeling miserable most of the time, I'm enjoying this reprieve, however short it may be.

One of the most respected Stanford humanities professors, Robert Harrison, called death the "culmination" of life. He may be thinking of "culmination" in the Catholic sense of making peace with God and receiving the last rites. Can the idea of culmination have meaning for someone who is not a religious believer? If I can avoid the misery of too much physical pain, if I can enjoy the simple pleasures of living from day to day, if I can say farewell to my dearest friends—either in person or writing—if I can rise to my best self and express my love for them and, with grace, accept my fate, then, perhaps, the moment of dying will be a form of culmination.

I think back to the ways death has been viewed throughout history, or at least the history I know. I recall, from my book *The Amorous Heart*, a vivid picture from the Egyptian Book of the Dead. The ancient Egyptians, more than three thousand years ago, judged the passage from life to death in a most dramatic manner. The heart, considered the seat of the soul, would be weighed on a scale. If it were pure enough and weighed less than the feather of truth, the deceased would gain entry into the afterlife. But if it were heavy with evil deeds, it would sink lower on the scale than the feather and cause the dead man or woman to be devoured by a grotesque beast.

Well, even if I don't believe literally in that kind of judgment, I do believe that dying persons—when they have time to reflect—tend to evaluate the lives they have lived. Certainly that is my case. And without being self-satisfied in a negative sense, I feel that I have caused no harm and can come to my end with few regrets and little guilt. The many emails, cards, and letters I have received keep telling me that I was helpful in significant ways to a number of people. That is certainly one of the reasons that I feel calm most of the time and can anticipate the possibility of a "good death."

A concern with dying well goes back to the Greek and Roman authors Seneca, Epictetus, and Marcus Aurelius. Each tried to make sense of a universe in which any individual existence was seen as a miniscule crack of light between two eternities of darkness, one before life and one afterwards. Advising the best ways to live both socially and rationally, these philosophers wanted us not to fear death, but to accept its inevitability in the great scheme of things.

Although Christian visions of God and an afterlife supplanted the thoughts of these "pagan" writers, the idea of dying well has hung on over the centuries and continues to influence the titles of several recent books, such as *The Art of Dying Well* by Katy Butler (2019). Sherwin Nuland's *How We Die: Reflections on Life's Final Chapter* (1995) presents a frank and compassionate account of how life departs from the body.

Of course, as Dr. P. reminds me, dying is always an individual affair; there is no one death to fit everyone, even for people with the same disease. I may just get progressively weaker or one of my organs will give out or, if I need heavy sedation, I may die painlessly in my sleep. Since I have the option of physician-assisted suicide, while I am still lucid and can express my wishes, I may set a date for my death. In addition to a hospice doctor and nurse, I will ask for my husband and children to be there at the time.

For now I am guided by the hospice staff, who are very attuned to the needs of dying patients. They seem to anticipate my questions even before I ask them and, based on their work with others who have died before me, they help me formulate answers. I can call Mission Hospice at any time of day or night to get directions for taking the medication which is already in my cabinet and refrigerator. They will send someone to the house in case of an emergency. We have already completed the paperwork that expressly declines extreme measures to keep me alive. In the end, however that comes, I should have some measure of control.

Still, even if I am not afraid of death itself, I feel the continued sadness of separating from my loved ones. For all the philosophical treatises and for all the assurances of the medical profession, there is no cure for the simple fact that we must leave each other.

CHAPTER 18

A SOOTHING ILLUSION

IT HAS NOW BEEN SIX WEEKS since Dr. M. opined that Marilyn had only one to two months to live. Despite this passage of time, Marilyn looks quite well and is very much alive. Our son Ben sent an email to the entire family saying: "Hello all—Despite her protests to the contrary, it looks like our dear mother will be around for Thanksgiving! She has asked that we all plan to gather in Palo Alto to celebrate."

Marilyn is currently listening to a taped lecture on Marcus Aurelius. She has had an excellent week: very little nausea, a bit of an appetite, and slightly more energy. She still spends much of the day lying on the living room couch, dozing or admiring the gigantic oak tree outside our window. And twice this week, she was willing to walk the hundred feet to the mailbox.

Marilyn's illness increases my awareness of my own mortality. I make some purchases from Amazon—double A batteries, ear plugs, Splenda—and select the same large amounts as I always had. Just before pressing the "buy" key, I chasten myself: "Irv, you can't order another shipment of thirty double A batteries or a box of 1,000 packets of Splenda. You're too old: no way you're going to live that long." I settle on a smaller, more thrifty order.

I have no higher pleasure than holding hands with Marilyn. I cannot get enough of her. It's been like this since junior high. People kidded us about always holding hands at lunchtime in the Roosevelt High School cafeteria—we're still doing it seventy years later. I struggle to hold back my tears as I write these words.

———

I hear Marilyn and our daughter, Eve, laughing and chattering away in one of the spare bedrooms. I'm curious about what they are doing and join them. They're going over Marilyn's jewelry—her rings, necklaces, and broaches, piece by piece, deciding who, among our children and grandchildren, in-laws and close friends, should inherit each piece. They appear to be enjoying their discussion.

Minutes pass and, though it is only 10 A.M., I grow fatigued and lie down on one of the beds as I continue watching. After a few more minutes, I begin to shiver. Even though the room is heated to 70 degrees, I pull the blanket over me. The entire scene feels macabre: I couldn't possibly imagine myself being so lighthearted as I give away all these markers of my life. Marilyn has a story about each piece— where she had gotten it or who had given it to her. I feel as though everything is vanishing. Death is devouring all of life, all of memory.

Eventually I am so overcome by grief I have to leave the room. Within minutes, I am back at my computer typing these words—as though this will forestall the passage of time. And isn't this entire book project serving the same purpose? I am trying to freeze time by painting the present scene and, hopefully, transporting it for some distance into the future. It's all illusion. But a soothing illusion.

CHAPTER 19

FRENCH BOOKS

I AM IN MY STUDY looking at empty shelves. These shelves used to hold my French books. There must have been at least six hundred books, stacked from ceiling to floor in two rows. Irv and I have been book people for as long as I can remember. We bonded over books when we were teenagers and have been immersed in books ever since. Our house brims with books, and I seem to be the only one who knows where most of them can be found, but even I have my lapses.

Yesterday Marie-Pierre Ulloa, my younger friend from the Stanford French Department, came with her husband, boxed up my French books, and carried them away. They will find a new home in her library and will be made available to scholars and students. It gives me comfort to know that these books will not be scattered to the wind.

And yet I am filled with grief. These books represent a significant part of my history, seventy years of immersion in French literature and culture. The oldest book—which I did not give away—is a copy of *Cyrano de Bergerac* presented to me by my French teacher, Mary Girard, when I graduated from high school in 1950. She wrote as an inscription:

À Marilyn, avec des souvenirs affectueux du passé et de très bons voeux pour l'avenir.

To Marilyn, with affectionate memories of the past and very good wishes for the future.

It was Madame Girard who suggested I go to Wellesley College, then known for its excellent French department, and that I also consider a career as a French teacher. Little did she (or I) suspect I would go on to get a PhD in comparative literature and become a professor of French for a good part of my life.

My books were arranged in historical order beginning with the Middle Ages at the top of the first shelf and ending at the bottom of the second row with a bevy of twentieth-century writers, such as Colette, Simone de Beauvoir, Violette le Duc, and Marie Cardinal. The shift from predominantly male writers in earlier centuries to more recent female writers probably represents my own taste, but also the increased prominence of women in literature today.

I remember the controversy about the new translation of de Beauvoir's *Second Sex* written by my good friends Constance Borde and Sheila Malovany-Chevallier. The translation was deemed "too literal" by some critiques, and I felt myself obliged to defend it in a letter to the *New York Times*. Their translation with an inscription to me is another book I could not part with.

But almost all the other books are now gone, leaving empty shelves and a great emptiness in my heart. Yet the thought that Marie-Pierre will share these books gives me hope that they will ripple into the lives of others. Marie-Pierre suggested that I affix book plates stating that these come from the library of Marilyn Yalom, so I have asked Irv to get them for me.

What will happen to my other books, including works of women's studies, life writing, German, and chess? I'll call some of my colleagues and ask them to take whatever they want. And I'll just have to leave such problems in the hands of Irv and the children. More and more, I have to assimilate that, when I die, I shall have no consciousness and no say in the matter.

———

Something quite unexpected has emerged from my connection with France, books, and my French friends. Last year when I was in Paris, I spent time with my good friends Philippe Martial and Alain Briottet. Both had spent World War II in the French countryside, Philippe in Normandy under German occupation and Alain in what was then called "the free zone" in the South. Alain had recently published a memoir about his officer father's captivity in German prison camps after the armistice of 1940.

I proposed to them that we edit a book entitled *Innocent Witnesses*, about children's memories of World War II, a book that would include our own stories, as well as others I would collect from friends. Childhood stories rarely focus exclusively on the terrors of war. Children remember what they

ate—or what they didn't eat, and especially the torments of
hunger. They remember the kindness of strangers who took
them into their homes and the rare toy given to them on their
birthday or at Christmas. They remember their play with
other children, some of whom disappeared from their lives
due to displacement or death. They remember the sound of
sirens and explosions and the bright flares that illuminated
the night sky. Children's eyes take in the everyday workings
of war, and when reopened through memory, help the rest
of us witness its brutal realities.

In *Innocent Witnesses*, I compile childhood histories from
six people whom I have come to know as colleagues and
friends, following first-person accounts and decades-long
conversations with them. I did not know these individuals
when we were children during the war. But, knowing them
all as adults, I marvel at their ability to transcend their pasts
and become thoughtful and accomplished adults. From their
memories, it is possible to speculate on the circumstances
that helped them survive. Which adult figures offered safety
and hope to guide them through the worst of times? What
personal qualities helped them become functioning adults?
How did they deal with their traumatic wartime memories?
Now that several of these people have passed away—and the
rest of us will undoubtedly be gone in the near future—I feel
a special obligation to communicate these stories.

As soon as I returned to California, I set to work immediately on the manuscript. Surprisingly, I got pretty far
along with it, even with the multiple myeloma diagnosis and
treatment. When I abandoned treatment, I decided to send
the manuscript to my agent, Sandy Dijkstra, to see if she
thought it was publishable.

Things then happened very quickly! Sandy sent material to Stanford University Press and within a week they made an excellent offer—not just to publish *Innocent Witnesses*, but also to publish this book with Irv. This feels like a gift from the gods. Now all I have to do is stay alive in order to work on the two books with my editor, Kate Wahl. She has already read the manuscript and made many suggestions. I hope I'm up to the work. With Thanksgiving just two weeks away and the children all coming here, I have to conserve whatever energy I can for them and for my *two* book projects.

CHAPTER 20

THE END APPROACHES

I AM OUT IN MY OFFICE much of the morning, a three-minute walk from the house, and am shocked when I enter Marilyn's office. Half of her bookshelves are empty. I hadn't been forewarned about this. Making her books available to students is entirely rational, but I know there is no way in the world I could have done as she has. I simply don't want to witness a preview of how my most meaningful possessions will vanish after my death.

This is a major reason I will resist moving into a smaller senior citizen dwelling: giving away my books feels too painful. I'll leave that task to my children: I can depend on them to make rational and intelligent decisions. Back in my office, I swivel my desk chair around and take a good look at the wall of books behind me. There are seven partitions each with seven shelves containing approximately thirty books—about 1,500 books in all. Though the arrangement of the books appears haphazard, it is intelligible to me. The first third are alphabetized by author. But the rest of the books are arranged by their relation to a book I have written: several shelves of books by and about Nietzsche, then shelves about Schopenhauer and others about Spinoza, about existential psychotherapy, about group therapy. As I survey them, they evoke my state of mind and my memory of where we were in the world while writing each book. Writing my stories and my novels was the high point of my life, and the exact place where certain charged ideas emerged remains vivid in my mind. I wrote several chapters of *When Nietzsche Wept* in the Seychelles, and *Love's Executioner* in Bali, Hawaii, and Paris. My group therapy textbook in London. Part of *The Schopenhauer Cure* in Austria and Germany.

Marilyn's equanimity at the sight of all her empty shelves is so very typical of her. There is no question that she experiences far less death anxiety (and less anxiety in general) than I, and I have little doubt about its source in our early lives. Let me tell you a story about our lives, a story that I believe sheds some light on the genesis of anxiety.

Marilyn's father, Samuel Koenick, and my father, Benjamin Yalom, emigrated after World War II, each from small shtetls in Russia, and each opened small grocery stores in Washington, DC. Marilyn's father had arrived in the US in late adolescence. He had a year or two of secular education in the US, after which he traveled as a free spirit around the country before he met and married Marilyn's mother, Celia, who had immigrated to the US from Poland. My father, on the other hand, arrived in the US at the age of 21 and had no secular education whatsoever.

Both of our fathers worked hard, rarely leaving their stores. My father's hours were longer since he sold liquor as well as groceries, and the store was open till 10 P.M. daily and midnight on Fridays and Saturdays.

More acclimated to US culture, Marilyn's father chose a house for his wife and three daughters in a genteel and safe part of Washington approximately a twenty-minute drive from the store, whereas my father decided that his family (my mother, my seven-years-older sister, and I) should live in the small apartment atop the grocery store in what was then considered an unruly and dangerous neighborhood. For my parents, choosing to live above the store made practical sense: my mother could relieve my father when he wanted to eat or take a rest. And when the stores was busy, he could phone my mother and she would rush down in a couple of minutes.

Though living atop the store was convenient for them, it proved disastrous for me: I rarely felt safe outside my home. I generally worked in the store on Saturdays and on school vacations—not because my parents requested it but because, aside from my voracious reading, there was little else I could find to do. Washington was then racially segregated, and we were the only white family in the neighborhood aside from other store owners. One of them, five blocks away, had been a close friend of my parents from the same shtetl in Russia. All my friends were black children, but my parents did not permit them to enter into our home. Moreover, the white children dwelling a few blocks away had already been schooled in anti-Semitism. Every day I walked the eight long and sometimes perilous blocks to Gage Elementary School which was located just within the border of a white section of the city. I recall being greeted on many days by the barber a few doors from my father's store with, "Hey, Jew boy—how's it going!"

After a few years my father gave up groceries and sold beer and liquor only. Though the store was more profitable, it also had a more unsavory set of customers and was subject to multiple robberies. For protection, my father hired an armed guard who sat in the back of the store. When I was 15, my mother insisted on buying a house and moving to a safer neighborhood. My life changed entirely: a better school, safer streets, and friendly neighbors. And most of all, I met Marilyn in the ninth grade. Though my life, from that point on, improved dramatically, even now, eighty years later, I'm still haunted by the anxiety generated in those early years.

Marilyn's early life could not have been more different. She grew up in a safe, pleasant part of the city. Neither Marilyn, her sisters, nor her mother ever set foot in the store. Moreover Marilyn attended elocution school, had music lessons, and encountered continual praise, no anti-Semitism, and no threats in her entire life.

It was only months after Marilyn and I met that we discovered our parents' stores were only a block apart. My father's store was on the corner of First and Seaton Streets and her father's store was on the corner of Second and Seaton Streets. As a child and adolescent, I must have walked or biked past my future father-in-law's store literally a thousand times! Our fathers, though, never laid eyes on one another until years after they retired and met at our engagement party.

Hence, from a distance, our early lives seem similar: parents who emigrated from Eastern Europe, fathers who had grocery stores only a block from one another. Yet, there were yawning differences in our early lives. Many of the early explorers in my field—Sigmund Freud, Anna Freud, Melanie

Klein, John Bowlby—concluded that early trauma, even dating back to preverbal eras, takes its toll, often an indelible toll, on the comfort, the ease, the self-esteem, of the adult, even into late stages of life.

CHAPTER 21

DEATH ARRIVES

IT IS THE GRIMMEST OF TIMES. Marilyn's death is now visible on the horizon, growing ever closer and permeating every decision, large and small. She drinks Earl Grey breakfast tea, and when I see there are only two tea bags remaining, I go to the grocery store to buy some more. But how many? No one else in the house drinks tea. There are twenty bags in each box. I fear she shan't be alive for more than a few more days, yet I purchase two boxes—forty tea bags—a magical plea to keep her with me a bit longer.

She wakes in the morning, complaining of pain in her back. She can hardly move without severe pain, and I do all I can to help her find a less painful position in her bed. She suffers terribly, and I feel miserably helpless.

I wonder why she no longer mentions ending her life: she spoke of it so often when she was in far less pain. Has she changed her mind? She knows the option to end her life is immediately available to her because, two days before, Dr. P.

drove over an hour to the nearest pharmacy that sold the lethal drug mixture and then delivered it to us. He placed it in the back of a small closet in our bathroom in a bag with large warning signs on it.

Her back pain is so severe she can no longer go downstairs even using the electric stair chair. Persuaded that her pain is exacerbated by the soft double bed Marilyn and I shared, the hospice nurse insists that Marilyn sleep in a firmer bed in the small bedroom across the hall. This night, Marilyn sleeps better, but I sleep poorly: I am so concerned that I might not hear her if she calls out in pain that I lay awake, listening, much of the night. The following day my children and I undertake a major furniture rearrangement and move the small firmer bed into our bedroom next to our double bed and move our huge bedroom bookcase into another room.

It is now obvious that Marilyn will be unable to enjoy Thanksgiving with the family. Her pain has increased so much that the hospice staff gives her a small dose of morphine every hour to make her more comfortable. The first two doses of morphine cause her to sleep much of the day. Whenever I try to talk to her, she can only mumble a few words before falling back asleep. Though I am happy that her pain is relieved, I weep when I realize that she and I may have already conversed together for the last time. I see also my son Ben's frustration. He has agreed to edit *Innocent Witnesses*, her book about childhood memories of World War II, but he cannot be certain which is the most recent version of the manuscript and tries several times to ask Marilyn about its location on her computer. But she is too groggy to respond.

Marilyn is often incontinent, and several times daily my daughter and my youngest son, Ben (who has three very young children and is highly experienced with soiled diapers), help clean and dress her. At such times I walk out of the room: I want to preserve my memory of my beautiful unsullied Marilyn. The rest of the day I remain by her side all day struggling still with the ghastly fact that we may have exchanged our last words with one another.

Late in the afternoon she suddenly opens her eyes, turns toward me, and speaks. "It's time. Irv, it's time. No more, please. No more. I don't want to live."

"Shall I ask Dr. P. to come?" I ask, my voice quavering. She nods vigorously.

Dr. P. arrives ninety minutes later, but he concludes that Marilyn is too obtunded from the morphine to voluntarily swallow the life-ending drugs, as California law requires. He leaves orders to sharply limit her morphine and informs us that he and his nurse will return the following morning at 11 A.M. He gives us his cell phone number and urges us to call him at any time if necessary.

The following morning Marilyn wakes at 6 A.M. very disturbed and again pleads for Dr. P. to help her end her life. We phone him, and he arrives within an hour. Marilyn had requested earlier that all of our children be present at her death. Three of our children had slept in our house this last night, but the other is at his home in Marin, an hour's drive away.

When my son arrives from Marin, Dr. P. leans close to Marilyn and asks in her ear, "What would you like?"

"No life. No more."

"Are you certain you want to end your life now?" he asks.

Though Marilyn is extremely groggy, she manages a clear firm nod.

Dr. P. first gives her some medication to prevent vomiting and then prepares the lethal drugs in two glasses. The first glass contains 100 milligrams of digoxin, enough to stop the heart. The second glass contains morphine 15 grams, amitriptyline 8 grams, and diazepam 1 gram.

He appears worried and, as he places straws in each glass, voices his concern: "I'm hoping she is conscious enough and strong enough to suck up the drug in the glass. The law demands that the patient be conscious enough to swallow the drug."

We help Marilyn sit up in bed. She opens her mouth for the straw and sucks up the glass of digoxin. Immediately Dr. P. holds up the second glass to her lips. Though Marilyn is too weak to speak, she readily sucks on the straw emptying that glass as well. She lays down on the bed, eyes closed, and breaths deeply. Surrounding the bed is Dr. P., the nurse, our four children, and me.

My head is next to Marilyn's head, and my attention riveted on her breathing. I watch her every movement and silently count her breaths. After her fourteenth feeble breath, she breaths no more.

I lean over to kiss her forehead. Her flesh is already cool: death has arrived.

My Marilyn, my darling Marilyn, was no more.

———

In less than an hour, two men from the funeral parlor arrive and we all wait downstairs. Fifteen minutes later, they carry her down the stairs in a shroud, and just before they walk out the front door, I ask to see her one more time. They unzip the top part of the shroud, expose her face, and I lean over and put my lips on her cheek. Her flesh was hard and very cold. That icy kiss will haunt me the rest of my life!

CHAPTER 22

THE AFTER-DEATH
EXPERIENCE

AFTER MARILYN'S BODY is taken away by the morticians, I remain in a state of shock. My mind keeps returning to our writing project, which has now become *my* writing project. Remember this scene, I tell myself. Remember everything that happens, everything that passes through my mind, so I can write about these final moments. Over and over, I hear me whispering to myself: *I shall never see her again, I shall never see her again, I shall never see her again.*

The funeral is the day after tomorrow. Though I'm surrounded by all four of my children and in-laws and many grandchildren, I feel more alone than ever before in my life. I weep silently as I climb the stairs and spend most of Marilyn's death day alone in my bedroom, trying to assuage my misery by observing the activity of my mind. Certain repetitive thoughts appear, intrusive and unwanted scenes which offer me a vivid and powerful experience of the obsessional mind. Again and again, I see in my mind scenes of the terrible Tiananmen

Square massacre and watch the huge army tanks crushing pro-
testing students in China. Indeed the thought is like a tank. I
cannot stop it. It thunders through my mind.

Why on earth this scene? I'm baffled. I hadn't thought
much about the Tiananmen uprising since it happened, some
thirty years ago. Perhaps it was touched off by the repeti-
tious recent television scenes of the current student riots in
Hong Kong. Perhaps it is a visual expression of the brutal
inexorability of death. One thing is certain: this scene is unwelcome—I do not want it contaminating my mind. I search
in vain for an off switch but to no avail: again and again the
same scene barrels into my mind. I've worked countless hours
with obsessional patients but now, at this moment, I have a
far more vivid and deep appreciation of their struggles. Prior
to this day I have never fully grasped how unwelcome and
unstoppable an obsession is. I try to push it out of my mind
by going through my mantra of breathing, inhaling while
saying "calm" and exhaling saying "ease," but to no avail. I
am amazed by my powerlessness: I can't do this more than
five or six breath cycles before I'm once again viewing the
merciless student-crushing tanks.

I feel exhausted and lie down in bed. My daughter and
daughter-in-law unexpectedly enter the room and lie down
next to me. They are gone when I awake three hours later—
perhaps the longest mid-day nap of my life and the very first
time I can recall sleeping on my back!

Several hours later, when I go to bed for the night, I feel
unmoored and unreal. This will be my first night without
Marilyn. The first of all my solitary nights until the end of
my life. Oh, I've had many nights without Marilyn as I lectured in other cities or when she was visiting Paris, but this

is the first night I've ever gone to sleep when there was no Marilyn, when Marilyn no longer existed. This night I sleep an unnaturally deep sleep for nine hours. When I awake, I realize that I have slept twelve out of the last twenty-four hours—the longest and deepest sleep in a twenty-four hour period that I can remember.

My four children, without asking me, effectively take over all the details of the events of the next few days, including arrangements with the funeral parlor, meeting with the rabbi and funeral parlor director, and selecting speakers as well as hiring caterers for the large post-funeral gathering at my home. This makes my life much easier, and I am very grateful and proud of them but, at the same time, there is a part of me, an ornery, childish part, that doesn't like being ignored. I feel overlooked, old, ineffectual, superfluous, discarded.

—————·

Burial day. The cemetery is directly across the street from Gunn High School, which all my children attended and approximately a twenty-five minute walk from my home. Though I write these words only a few days after Marilyn's death, relatively little of the funeral remains vivid in my mind. I have to talk to my children and friends to bring it to consciousness. Traumatic repression: another interesting psychological phenomenon that many patients have described to me that I had never before personally experienced.

I'll start with what I *do* recall with clarity. Someone (I don't remember who—but I suspect it was my daughter who hovered close to me the entire day) drives me to the chapel at the cemetery. I recall the spacious chapel is full already when we arrive ten minutes early. Patricia Karlin-Neuman, the rabbi whom we had met a few years ago when Marilyn and I had been invited to speak at the Hillel House at Stanford, opens the ceremony. There are brief eulogies by three of my children (Ben, Eve, and Reid) and two of our closest friends (Helen Blau and David Spiegel). I have a clear recollection that, without exception, each of the five presentations are superbly crafted and delivered. I am especially struck by my son Reid's talk. He's been an excellent photographer for most of his life, but only within the last year has he shown me the poetry and prose he had written about his childhood and adolescence. It's clear he has considerable talent that he has only recently tapped into. But this is all I recall of the funeral service. I've never before so extensively erased events from my memory (or failed to register them).

Next thing I recall, I am sitting outdoors next to the burial site. How did I get here from the auditorium in the funeral parlor? Did I walk? Or a short automobile ride? I don't remember. Later I ask my daughter who tells me that she and I walked over together. I do remember the grave site and sitting with my children in the front row of chairs directly in front of Marilyn's coffin which was slowly lowered into a deep trench. Just a few feet away is her mother's grave.

I recall being in a fog and sitting still as a statue. I can only vaguely recall all the guests lined up in front of the trench, and while a prayer is chanted, each person in turn picks up a shovel and tosses dirt upon the casket. I recall this tradition from other burials I have attended. But on this day, I am horrified by it, and I absolutely will not toss dirt onto Marilyn's coffin. So I just sit there, in a trance, until everyone is finished. I don't know whether anyone notices my refusal to participate in burying Marilyn, or if they do, I hope they might attribute it to my unsteadiness on my feet and my heavy reliance on my cane. Soon afterwards, I leave for home with my children.

At home many, perhaps most, of the folks at the service are enjoying conversation, champagne, and morsels of food provided by the caterer my children engaged. I cannot recall whether I drink or taste anything. I believe I speak at length to a couple of close friends, but again all other details of the reception have evaporated. Of one thing I am certain: I was not a proper host, circulating, greeting our friends; in fact I don't recall getting out of my chair. Sitting next to me, two friends speak of attending an upcoming evening Stanford course on the nineteenth- and twentieth-century short story and invite me to join them.

Oh, yes, I'll do that, I decide. Perhaps this represents the beginning of my life without Marilyn.

And then, almost instantly, I begin thinking of her in her coffin underground. But I banish that thought: I know Marilyn is *not* there in her coffin. She is not *anywhere*. She no longer exists—except in my memory and in the memory of all the many people who loved her. Will I ever really grasp this? Will I ever come to terms with her death? And of my death to come?

I do not have to face Marilyn's death alone: after the funeral my four dear children stay with me as long as they can. My daughter, Eve, takes off from her work as a gynecologist for almost three weeks and takes loving care of me. Finally I tell her I feel I am ready to be alone, but on her very last night with me, I have a bona fide nightmare, my first in a great many years. It's dark, the middle of the night, and I hear a creaking sound. I know that the bedroom door is opening. I turn toward the doorway and see a man's head. He's handsome, and he is wearing a dark grey fedora. Somehow I know he's a gangster, and I also know he's going to kill me. I wake up with my heart pounding.

The one obvious message of this dream is that I, too, have an impending engagement with death. That gray fedora . . . my father wore a grey fedora like that. And my father was handsome. But far from a gangster. He was a kind and gentle man who died over forty years ago. Why am I dreaming of my father? I rarely think of him. Perhaps he's not sent to kill me, but to escort me to the realm of the dead where Marilyn and I shall forever reside.

Perhaps the dream is also telling me I am not yet prepared for my daughter to leave, not ready to be alone. But I do not share this dream with her: she's a physician and has already cancelled many appointments with her patients. It is time for her to return to her own life. My son Reid may have picked up that I am not ready to be alone and without asking me comes to spend the following weekend. We enjoy many chess games just as we had when he was a child.

It is not until the following week, when Marilyn has been dead for a month, that I spend my first weekend alone. As I look back onto Marilyn's funeral, I wonder about my feeling so numb and calm on the day of burial. Perhaps it stems from my having been so close to her as she lay dying. I left nothing undone. I rarely left her side and counted the last breaths she took. And that last kiss on her icy cheek—*that* was the real moment of saying goodbye.

Holding hands at our engagement party.

WE WILL REMEMBER

Eulogies for Marilyn Yalom

NOVEMBER 22

Eve Yalom, daughter

Very early on, when my mother was going through chemo-therapy, she received an outpouring of love from so many of you. She frequently said that she realized that "You don't live just for yourself." Until this journey she really didn't appreciate how important she was to so many of you—how many of you had been mentored, mothered, encouraged, pushed, and loved by her.

This realization deeply affected her and made her last few months worth living. She wanted to say goodbye person-ally to everyone and let each of you know how much she loved you.

As her child I took for granted that there was always room for another plate on the table, another centimeter of space on my mother's tiny but mighty lap. I felt profoundly loved, and mentored and, yes, pushed to be the best I could, as we all were.

How lucky was I to have had a mother who was such a feminist! It was lucky for my generation to know that it could be done, and lucky to be able to have guidance from her. And she mentored and mothered my childhood playmates and my children and their childhood playmates as well.

My life's work as an obstetrician has been of bringing new life into the world yet somehow it seems so fitting I am here to help shepherd her out.

Reid Yalom, son

Marilyn loved the earth,
loved to put her hands in the rich clay soil
kneeling to plant tomatoes
and harvest strawberries.
We will miss her apricot chutney and jams.
Marilyn loved the air.
A fine walker she was
on her sturdy legs.
I recall a special time
picking blueberries in Heidelberg
inhaling the blue scent.
And another moment,
watching her hold Irv's hand
on a Hawaiian beach at sunset.
I can see her close her eyes
and inhale
the salt-laden air.
She loved fire
and all things warm.
When winter wood crackled

Marilyn would always sit
singe-worthy close.
I remember that week at Silver Lake
when 3 generations gathered
for walks and swims.
and stories and songs
at the campfire
where she liked her marshmallows
browned evenly.
Marilyn loved beauty—
not in a simple hedonistic way,
but rather as life affirming,
as emblematic of humanity's goodness.
In a sense, it was goodness
that was her cause,
her religion.
She searched for it in her work
and shared it with the world—
in her writings,
and with her children
in everyday moments—
before dinner listening to
Vivaldi's Four Seasons,
perhaps a glass of not-too-dry sherry in hand—
or in extraordinary ways—
transporting us to behold
the stained-glass windows at Chartres—
but most importantly,
by her gathering such an amazing flock of friends,
students, colleagues—
and of course her family—
Irv, my siblings, our wives and her now

8 grandchildren.
She encouraged us all
to embrace her cause;
to find goodness
in other cultures, and religions,
in humanity.
in each other.
I will deeply miss her holding this light,
but I do not expect to see it diminished;
rather, to increase in intensity
radiating outwards into the night sky
like so many bright stars
in an ever-expanding universe.
Each of you now holds this light.

Our wedding. Washington, DC. June 1956.

Family gathering, 1976. Our daughter, Eve, and our sons
Reid, Victor, and Ben (sitting on the floor).

Ben Yalom, son

My mother had a particular way of seeing the world. This
was very much influenced by her time in France. *La façon
ou manière correcte de faire les choses.* The correct way of
doing things. This included polite, courteous speech, proper
manners, and brushing hair, washing hands, and putting on
a decent shirt for dinner. Beyond dealing with children, I
think this sense of *la façon correcte de faire les choses,* while
perhaps slightly out of place in late twentieth-century California, gave her confidence in the world, a sense of direction
that many of you have alluded to in the wonderful memories
you have shared.

One extreme of this world view was the expression, with which she regaled me often when I was young, that "Children should be seen and not heard." Ha! Much to her dismay, I was not a quiet, polite child. On the contrary, I was stubborn, full of needs, and very vocal. I don't remember being terribly difficult, but everyone assures me that I was.

I have been especially aware of this recently, watching her with my 6-year-old son, Adrian. He is a wild and deeply stubborn child. Quick to shout and throw things and assure me without a doubt that I am the worst father in the world, he is clearly my personal karmic comeuppance.

And yet, when calm, he is also beautiful and radiant and lovely. I used to fear my mother would be shocked by his behavior, so far as it often is from *la façon correct de fair les choses*, and so far as he is from being seen, not heard. On the contrary, Marilyn quickly developed a strong bond with him. *"Il est très attachant,"* she told me every time we spoke—one quickly becomes attached to him.

Together they would spend hours reading Mother Goose nursery rhymes—*Humpty Dumpty*, and *Four and Twenty Blackbirds*, and best of all (and over and over again):

Hey Diddle Diddle
the Cat and Fiddle
the Cow jumped over the Moon
the little Dog laughed to see such a sight
and here they would burst into laughter and shout out—
And the Dish Ran Away with the Spoooooooooon!

which would inevitably send Adrian rolling onto the floor in an uncontrollable fit of giggles.

Dancing in Hawaii for our fiftieth wedding anniversary.

This patience and warmth and tender joy reminds me that my mother was not, in fact, overly stern or strict, even though it sometimes seemed that way. Rather she managed to soothe that stubborn monster in me, somehow in her own calm, quiet, and wise way.

I know during these last months she spoke to each of her children, and many of her friends, sharing special memories. On Monday night, the last time we spoke lucidly, she told me—"You were my baby, you'll always be my baby."

We Will Remember
Read by Eve Yalom and her daughters Lily and Alana
Recited by everyone in attendance

When we smell the scent of lavender du Provence,
           We will remember her.
When we read an intelligent and well-crafted book,
           We will remember her.
When we refer to God in her female form,
           We will remember her.
When we women take a seat at the table
   and speak our minds,
           We will remember her.
When we feel reverence for history but feel free
   to question the patriarchy,
           We will remember her.
When we hear the bells of Saint Sulpice,
           We will remember her.
When the apricots are in bloom,
           We will remember her.
When afternoon tea becomes evening sherry,
           We will remember her.
When the prime rib is gnawed to the bone,
           We will remember her.
When the grammar police issue a citation,
           We will remember her.
When a champagne toast is lifted,
           We will remember her.
When we are confused, downcast, uplifted, or joyous,
           We will remember her.
As long as we live, she too will live, for she is now
   a part of us.
           We will remember her.

On a lecture trip in Russia.

CHAPTER 23

LIFE AS AN INDEPENDENT, SEPARATE ADULT

I TAKE FORTY-FIVE MINUTE walks every day, sometimes with friends or neighbors, but generally alone, and I spend several hours each day working on this book, as well as working many hours on the phone with my good friend and co-author, Molyn Leszcz, writing and editing the very last chapters of the forthcoming sixth edition of *The Theory and Practice of Group Psychotherapy*. Most of the time I feel busy and don't welcome many intrusions. So devoted am I to writing this book that I'm eager to get to my studio at about 8 A.M. every morning. I'm happiest when writing, but I worry about my state of mind when I have finished this work. My prediction is that deep sadness will descend upon me.

All in all, I'm astounded that I'm doing so well. Why haven't I been crippled by my loss? I never doubt the depth of my love for Marilyn: I feel certain that no man has ever loved a woman more. How many times, as I watched her suffer during the last few months, did I say to her, "I wish I could take your illness for you." And I meant it: I would have given my life for her.

I replay over and over again those horrific last thirty-six hours of her life when I never left her side and countless times kissed her forehead and cheeks even though she was often unresponsive. Her death was a release for both of us—for her a release from continual nausea, pain, severe fatigue from saying goodbye to the vast numbers of friends and family who love her. And for me a release from several months of helplessly watching her suffer. The last thirty-six hours were the worst for me because the morphine and lorazepam she received, even in small doses, hampered her ability to communicate: I tried to converse with her when she opened her eyes briefly, smiled at me, tried to say a word or two, and then drifted off. I recall being irrationally angry at the hospice nurse for giving too much morphine, thus depriving me of my last opportunity to speak with Marilyn.

Another farewell scene from the distant past unexpectedly flits into mind, a scene that occurred during the years I worked with groups of patients with terminal cancer—a scene I had long forgotten. On several occasions patients too ill to attend the group meeting would contact me requesting a house visit, to which I always agreed. One day I received such a request from Eva, a middle-aged women dying from ovarian cancer who had rarely missed a group meeting. I appeared at the front door of her home the day after I received her call, and her caretaker admitted me and led me to her bedroom. Eva, who had been dozing, smiled broadly when she saw me and, in a weak and gravelly voice, requested privacy. Her caretaker left the room.

She appeared very fragile, her once powerful voice now reduced to a whisper. She said that her doctor told her she had not much longer to live and advised her to go to the hospital, but she had refused, saying that she preferred to die at home. She then turned her head toward me, reached out for my hand and, looking straight into my eyes, said, "Irv, one final request please. Would you lie down in bed next to me?"

I could not possibly refuse her—I would never forgive myself—even though I was haunted by the image of defending myself to the dour and severe faces of a medical ethics panel. Without removing my shoes, I lay on my back next to her and while holding hands, we spoke for about twenty-five minutes and said farewell to one another. I feel proud for having offered this dear woman some comfort.

As this memory evaporates, my mind shifts back to Marilyn lying in her coffin deep underground. But I cannot, will not, stay focused on the cemetery or on her coffin—I know my darling Marilyn is not really there.

I believe I feel the sadness lifting. Perhaps chaos and despair are done with me. But a short time later I receive an email from Pat Berger. Her husband, Bob Berger, and I had been the closest of friends during and after our medical student days, right until he died three years ago. Toward the end of his life, we co-authored a book, *I'm Calling the Police*, about his survival in Hungary during the Nazi Holocaust. Pat Berger's email contains a beautiful photo of Marilyn taken three years ago under a flowering magnolia stalk. Looking at that photo and our past happy times ignites my pain and yanks me back to reality. I have no doubt that I have a great deal of suffering ahead of me.

Though I'm now in my eighty-eighth year, I still have much to learn about life—mainly how to live as an independent, separate adult. I've done so much in my life—becoming a doctor, taking care of so many patients, teaching students, writing books, fathering and raising four loving, generous, and creative children—*but I've never lived as an independent adult!* Yes, it's shocking but it's true. I astonish myself and I keep repeating it: *I have never lived as an independent adult.*

After we met in junior high school, Marilyn and I were always together until she boarded the train to attend Wellesley College in Massachusetts. I remained in Washington, DC, taking the premed curriculum at George Washington University, living with my parents, and doing nothing but intensive and anxious studying.

I had good cause for anxiety: at that time all US medical schools had a fixed 5 percent quota for Jewish students. I'm not sure of my source, but somewhere I learned that medical schools occasionally accepted outstanding students after only three years rather than four years of college. That was important information to me: I was in such a great rush to marry Marilyn and so threatened by all the Harvard students she was dating who had so much more to offer her—so much sophistication, so much wealth, so much family prominence. I grasped at the opportunity to shorten my time away from her and was absolutely determined to enter medical school a year earlier. The solution was obvious: if I got all A's during my three years as a GW undergraduate student, they would *have* to accept me into the GW Medical School. That was exactly what happened!

During our college years apart, Marilyn and I stayed in close touch: without fail we wrote letters every single day and occasionally spoke on the phone. (Long-distance phone calls from Washington to New England were expensive in those days, and I had no income whatsoever.)

Once admitted to George Washington Medical School, I stayed only one year before transferring to Boston University Medical School in order to be closer to Marilyn. There I rented a room in a house on Marlborough Street where four other medical students lived. I spent every weekend with Marilyn. We married in my third year of medical school and then lived together for the rest of Marilyn's life: first a flat in Cambridge, then a year in New York where I interned and three years at Johns Hopkins in Baltimore, followed by two years in Hawaii serving in the army, and then to Stanford in Palo Alto, California, for the rest of our lives.

So now, at the age of 88 and Marilyn dead, I find myself living alone for the very first time. I have to change so many things. If I see an outstanding TV show, I long to tell Marilyn about it, and over and again I have to remind myself that there *is* no Marilyn and that this TV show, this flake of life, is of value and interest even though Marilyn shall never share it. Analogous events happen very frequently. A woman phones and asks to speak to Marilyn. When I inform her of Marilyn's death, she begins sobbing on the phone, tells me how much she would miss Marilyn, and how important Marilyn had been to her. After the call ends, once again I have to remind myself that this experience, too, ends right now with me. There would be no sharing the experience with Marilyn.

But I am *not* referring to loneliness. It's a matter of learning that something can have value and interest and importance *even if I am the only one who experiences it, even if I cannot share it with Marilyn.*

———

A couple of days before Christmas, my entire extended family is in my home—my four children, their spouses, six grandchildren and their spouses—about twenty in all sleeping in every bedroom, living room, Marilyn's office, my office. My children are talking of the evening's menu and activities, and suddenly I freeze: I can hear them but cannot move. I feel like a statue, and my children grow more and more concerned. "Dad, are you okay? Dad, what's wrong?"

And then, for the first time, I burst into tears and try, with much difficulty, to say, "She's not here, not anywhere. Marilyn will *never, never* know of all that's happening here tonight." My children seem in shock: never before had they seen me weep.

Everyone feels Marilyn's absence keenly as the family assembles at our Christmas/Hanukah celebration. There are so many of us that we bring in Chinese food from a nearby restaurant for Christmas Eve. As we wait for dinner to appear, I finish a chess game with Victor. There's a bit of a lull, and I suddenly set out to say something to Marilyn. Of course, she's not there. I was engrossed in my game with my son, but now that the game is over, I suddenly feel empty. With the exception of her junior year in college abroad in France, I've spent every Christmas Eve with Marilyn for seventy consecutive years. I have feelings and nonverbal memories of all the other Christmases we have had together—all the trees, the presents, the singing and cooking. But this year is different: there is little cheer and no Christmas tree. I feel so chilly and cold that I stand on the hot air vent to feel better. I love everyone here very much—I am surrounded by my children and grandchildren—but I feel an emptiness. The center is missing.

On Christmas day, my daughter cooks the main course of Peking duck; others cook a variety of dishes that have no relationship with one another. Everyone knows, and many comment, that if Marilyn had been alive, we could never have gotten away with take-out food for Christmas Eve or dishes that don't go together for Christmas day dinner. Moreover, Marilyn always began the Christmas/Hanukah dinner with some formal remark or, generally, a Bible reading. On this first holiday without her, we all feel lost. There is no formal beginning: we simply sit down and eat. I miss the ceremonial reading: I just took it for granted like so many other things my precious wife provided for me.

For the last ten years, since she was sixteen, my granddaughter Alana and I have baked kichel on Christmas, following my mother's recipe. Alana is all grown up now, a fourth-year medical student, engaged to be married, and she is now the take-charge member of the kichel baking team. She and I prepare the dough and yeast and butter the night before, and early in the morning roll out the risen dough and add raisins, nuts, sugar, and cinnamon to create about thirty succulent pastries. This time we prepare them sadly, both of us thinking of how much Marilyn would have loved them.

The family has grown so large that for the past couple of Christmases we've drawn lots and each person buys one person a present. But this year we cancel present buying: there is too much sorrow and too little interest in giving or receiving gifts.

I'll have the children with me the next few days, so I'm not worried about loneliness. Lots of conversation, wonderful meals, much chess and Scrabble and pinochle. When the children all leave, I spend New Year's Eve alone. It turns out to be an unexpectedly benign experience. My introversion subdues loneliness. As midnight approaches, I switch on the TV and watch all the celebrations from Times Square to San Francisco. I suddenly realize this is only the second New Year's in *seventy years* that I'm without Marilyn by my side. (The first time was when she took her junior year in France.) On the TV, I see all the people cheering at Times Square, but I turn down the sound. There's no more Marilyn and real life is over. I feel heavy and sad, and I know that no one can fix this. Marilyn is dead. I imagine her decaying body in the coffin. She now lives only in my mind.

CHAPTER 24

HOME ALONE

EVERYWHERE I TURN reminders of Marilyn confront me. I enter our bedroom and see many of her medications on the table next to her side of the bed. Tomorrow I will ask Gloria, my housekeeper, to put them somewhere out of sight. Then I see a pair of Marilyn's reading glasses in her chair in the TV room, and several other pairs in her bathroom. Why did she have so many glasses? Along with endless bottles and boxes of medication, next to the sofa where she spent much of her last weeks, I spot her iPhone. What to do with all that? As with most things now, I avoid the problem and turn it over to my children.

Many weeks passed before I brought myself to open the door of her study. Even now, six weeks after her death, I do not venture far into the room and avoid looking at all the objects on her desk. I still don't want to touch Marilyn's possessions—I don't want to keep them—I don't want to dispose of them. Yes, I'm being infantile—but I don't care. I experience shame only when I think of all the bereaved folks I've counseled over the years who didn't have the luxury of a large family to remove all traces of the person who died.

A photo of Marilyn sits in a corner in the living room facing the wall. I saw this magnificent photo in her *Washington Post* obituary and liked it so well that I tracked down the negative and asked my son Reid, an accomplished photographer, to make a print. He framed it and brought it for Christmas. For the first few days, I made a point of gazing at the photo often, but, without exception, I experienced much pain and eventually turned the photo to the wall. Once in a while, I walk over to it, turn it over, take a deep breath and stare right at it. She is so beautiful, her lips seem to utter, "*Don't forget me . . . you and I, my darling, always . . . don't forget me.*" I turn away, heavy with pain. More pain than I can bear. I weep aloud. I don't know what to do.

Shall I protect myself from such pain? Or shall I do the opposite and persist in looking at her intensely and weeping over and again? I know there will come a time when I will hang that photo on the wall and will gaze at it with great pleasure. Our eyes will meet and lock, and we shall both be so full of love for the other and so grateful that we were able to spend our lives together. My tears flow as I type these lines and I stop, dab my eyes, and stare through our window at the branches of our oak tree stretching toward the clear blue sky.

Incidents abound that I wish to share with Marilyn. I learn that Maximart, our small neighborhood pharmacy that we have patronized for over forty years, has just closed for good, and immediately I imagine myself telling Marilyn this news and her subsequent disappointment. Or, our two oldest sons who, for years, had declined to play chess against one another, now amiably played chess during the Christmas holidays. Or, one of my sons, who had declined to learn pinochle, is now learning the rules and beginning to play with his brothers and me. Both the chess and the pinochle episodes reflect how the family is huddling closer together. Oh, how I wish I could tell that to Marilyn! She would have been so pleased.

As I read about other grieving individuals, I learn about the great diversity of behavior. I read a brief article by a bereaved husband who has an old voice message from his wife on his phone to which he repeatedly listens. I wince as I read that: I couldn't bear the pain of listening to Marilyn's voice. I wonder if it freezes him in grief and blocks him from starting some new life. But, then perhaps I'm taking too severe a stance. Everyone grieves in their idiosyncratic fashion.

I read an article that shows evidence that men who have lost their wives have a much higher mortality rate over the next four years than nonbereaved men. The prognosis is even worse for men who were highly dependent on the deceased wife for pleasure or esteem. Yet I'm untroubled by that: it is odd now how little concern I now have about my own death. I've often, too often, experienced death anxiety in past eras. I particularly recall nightmares about dying many years ago when I was working with therapy groups for patients dying from cancer. But, now not a trace of it. I am entirely unfazed by the thought of my death.

CHAPTER 25

SEX AND GRIEF

IT SEEMS LIKE AGES AGO that I was visited by those nightmarish images of armored tanks crushing students at Tiananmen Square, though it was only shortly after Marilyn died, while I awaited her funeral and burial. The persistence of those images gave me a new appreciation of the nature and the power of obsessional thinking. And after a few days, the armored tanks and Tiananmen Square gradually evaporated. My resting mind has grown more tranquil over the past weeks.

But, now, a new obsession has invaded my thoughts: whenever I relax and try to clear my mind, for instance awaiting sleep after turning out the lights, I am visited by enticing sexual thoughts involving women I've known or seen recently. These images are powerful and persistent. I try to block them, purge them from consciousness, turn my thoughts elsewhere. But, a few minutes later, they reappear and again seize my attention. I am flooded with both desire and shame. I wince at such disloyalty to Marilyn, buried only a few weeks ago.

As I look back over the last few weeks, I've also become aware of a curious (and embarrassing) development: intensified interest in women's breasts, especially sizable breasts. I don't know if any women have noticed this, but I have to keep reminding myself to look at the faces rather than the breasts of Marilyn's many friends who visit. A cartoon image comes to mind—I have no idea where I first saw it, perhaps in adolescence: I see a woman tugging a man's chin upwards toward her face as she says, "Yoo-hoo, I'm up here!"

This renewed interest is sometimes accompanied by a scene from the past—approximately seventy-five years ago—which, over the past few days, has often floated into my mind. In the scene, I recall myself as a 10- or 11-year-old, entering my parents' bedroom for some reason and encountering my mother who was only half dressed. Rather than covering herself, she stood there bare breasted and boldly stared into my eyes as though to say, "Take a good look!"

I recall, ages ago, spending a great many hours discussing this memory with Olive Smith, who was my analyst for over 600 hours of psychoanalysis during my psychiatric residency. Obviously I'm now in great distress, and it is no coincidence that I've regressed. Like a child, I am plaintively seeking maternal succor. A phrase that I've used somewhere in one of my books returns to mind, "Freud wasn't wrong about everything."

I am unsettled and ashamed of these sexual obsessions. A debate proceeds in my mind. How could I so dishonor myself and my love for Marilyn? Is this really how shallow my love is? *But, on the other hand, isn't it my task now to stay alive, to begin a new life?* Yet, I feel such shame about tarnishing Marilyn's memory. *But perhaps such sexual thoughts are perfectly natural for one who has been paired his entire life and suddenly finds himself single.*

I decide to examine the literature on bereavement and sexuality but, as the reader may recall, I am not on the best of terms with contemporary medical library research. I locate an expert in medical literature search—the same person who had recently assisted me and Molyn Leszcz, the co-author of the fifth and the sixth edition of our text book on group therapy. I assign her the task of searching the medical and psychological literature for any articles on bereavement and sexuality. A day later she emails me and replies she has searched for several hours but found zip . . . nothing . . . in the literature! She is apologetic and writes that, since she had nothing to show for her labor, she would refuse payment from me. "Nonsense," I reply, and insist on paying. Her inability to find any articles is important information in itself.

I then turn to a research assistant at Stanford, highly recommended by a close friend and colleague, and ask him also to spend a few hours researching the matter. Almost the identical scenario occurred: he finds virtually nothing in the medical and psychological literature, and I also have to insist that he accept payment for his time.

In the following days, however, both of these research assistants begin sending me a few more clinically based articles from more popular publications, for example, an article in *Psychology Today* (November 2015) entitled "5 Things They Don't Tell You About Grief" (written by Stephanie A. Sarkis, a practicing clinician). The fifth item in the article pertains explicitly to sexuality in grief:

Your sexual drive may actually increase. For many, grief decreases the sex drive. For many others, it can increase it. This can be especially conflicting for those who have lost a spouse or partner. But when people are numb from grief, they find that sex helps them feel *something*. It's also life-affirming at a time when coping with death has become part of one's everyday life.

Several thoughts in these lines hit home for me, especially the statement that when one is numb from grief, sex helps one feel something. "Numb" is an accurate term for what I've been experiencing: a sense of great distance from my feelings. I go through the motions of conversation, dining, watching TV whilst all the time not really being there. But the sexual thoughts feel more real, resulting in a life-affirming feeling that awakens me and rousts me from my preoccupation with death.

I have discussions with several experienced colleagues who work with grieving individuals, and they agree that sexual arousal and preoccupation among the bereaved is far more common than generally thought, often more an issue for men than women though, without question, it is an issue for women as well. The clinicians agree with my observation that clients will rarely initiate a discussion about increased feelings of sexuality. But, if practitioners *inquire explicitly* about problems around sexuality, a great many of the bereaved will respond positively. It seems that most bereaved individuals are ashamed and disinclined to raise the topic spontaneously. Consequently a great many of the personal accounts of grief avoid the topic or contain only a few oblique references pertaining to sexuality.

I conclude, with some relief, that my aroused state of mind is not rare, and without doubt, sexual longing plays a significant role in grief. Moreover, it is not easy for the elderly to be open about their inner sexual life. They don't feel at ease sharing it with family or friends. They dread making others uncomfortable. I am fortunate to have my therapists' group with whom I have been regularly meeting for decades. My discussion in that forum helps to temper my discomfort.

CHAPTER 26

UNREALITY

MY SON BEN VISITED with his three children, aged 6, 4, and 2. One evening I saw my three grandchildren glued to the television set, watching some gory animated children's program featuring monsters, young children, beasts, and miraculous escapes. Disgusted by it, I pre-emptively changed channels and searched for another show. I soon fell upon a lively production of animated figures dancing to the Nutcracker Suite. Despite groans and complaints from my grandchildren, I stayed tuned to that channel. After a few minutes, mirabile dictu, the groans stopped and all three watched the Nutcracker Suite with much interest. Delighted and aching to share this with Marilyn, I stopped the TV for a few seconds to hit the record button so that Marilyn could see it herself. I turned the play button back on, and the children watched joyously.

Only a couple of minutes later it hit me. *I was astonished. What am I doing? Recording this for Marilyn to watch?*

Marilyn is dead I remind myself! A great many similar episodes have occurred.

———

Recently, a friend told me that Bell's Bookstore in downtown Palo Alto was prominently displaying several of my books and Marilyn's books on a table by the front entrance. The following day I stopped at the bookstore with my iPhone in hand to take a picture for Marilyn to see. Not until I'm walking down the street toward the bookstore does the truth—*Marilyn is dead*—hit me once again.

———

A couple of months before Marilyn died, she and I took a stroll up our street and saw a new neighbor, a distinguished white-haired elderly man, obviously handicapped, being helped down the front stairs of his home and into an automobile by a younger dark-skinned woman who, no doubt, we assumed, was his caretaker.

The day after Christmas, these new neighbors (whom I still had not yet met) invited me to dinner and Christmas carols. I arrived at the house and was greeted by the elderly man and the caretaker. I soon learned that he was a retired MD and that the "caretaker" had an MD and a PhD degree! Moreover, she was not his caretaker but his wife! She was delightful and led the Christmas carols with a glorious voice! Again, my first thought: *wait till I tell Marilyn about this!* Even now I regret not being able to share this with Marilyn.

———

Last night I learned that the third season of the BBC TV show, *The Crown*, had started. Marilyn and I had watched the first and second seasons a couple of years ago. So I began watching the third season and was deeply engrossed in it. I enjoyed watching the first couple of episodes, but scenes of episode three seemed oddly familiar. After checking more closely, I discovered that I had not been watching the third season at all, but episodes of the first season which I had already seen. I felt the urge to tell Marilyn—quickly followed by the return to reality: Marilyn will *never* know about this incident. She was concerned, sometimes vexed, about my porous memory. But I could also imagine her amusement and her dancing eyes, hearing that I had watched three hours of a program before realizing I had already seen it. As I write these words, I feel a clutch in my chest. I'd give anything . . . *anything* . . . to see that smile on her face.

———

I receive a letter from my agent, reminding me that some time ago we had granted a Romanian screenwriter the permission to write a screenplay of my novel, *The Spinoza Problem*. The project has now morphed into a ten-hour episodic TV series with a 400-page script that needs to be broken down into episodes. Again my first thought is "Oh, I can hardly wait to tell Marilyn" until, seconds later, dark reality sets in. I am left holding the incident, joyless and alone. It's as if Marilyn's knowing about a happening is necessary to make it truly real.

I've been a full-time student, observer, and healer of the mind for over sixty years, and it is difficult to tolerate my own mind being so irrational. My patients sought my help for an enormous range of issues—for problems with relationships, for greater self-understanding, for disturbing feelings from depression, mania, anxiety, loneliness, anger, jealousy, obsessions, unrequited love, for nightmares, phobias, agitation—that is, the whole range of human psychological difficulties. I acted as a guide in helping my clients achieve self-understanding, to clarify their fears, their dreams, their past and present relationships with others, their inability to love, their anger. Underlying this entire endeavor is the truism that we are capable of rational thinking and that understanding ultimately brings relief.

Hence, my sudden irrational episodes are highly disturbing. To encounter some part of my mind that obstinately continues to believe that Marilyn is still alive is astounding and unsettling. I've always scoffed at irrational thinking, at all the mystical notions about heaven and hell and what happens after death. My group therapy textbook presents a rational approach based on my delineation of twelve therapeutic factors. *The Gift of Therapy*, my text on individual therapy, contains eighty-five clearly described tips for therapists. My existential therapy textbook is structured around four major existential factors—death, freedom, isolation, and meaning in life. Rationality and clarity are major reasons why my books are used in so many classrooms around the world. And, yet, here I am today experiencing so many irrational moments!

I speak of my discomfort about my irrational thinking to a former student, now a professor of psychiatry and a neurobiologist who responds that memory is no longer believed to be a unitary phenomenon; rather, memory is comprised of distinct systems that can work independently, have different neuroanatomic loci, and can even work at odds with each other. He describes the dichotomy between "explicit" (or "declarative") memory versus "implicit" (or "procedural") memory.

Explicit memory is conscious and is dependent on medial temporal lobe structures as well as the cortex of the brain. It involves the formation and conscious retrieval of memories of events that have occurred (e.g., "I consciously know that Marilyn has passed away."). *Implicit memory* is largely unconscious and often underlies skills, habits, and other automatic behaviors. It is processed in different parts of the brain: the basal ganglia for skills, the amygdala for emotional responses. So my recent painful explicit memory that Marilyn has died is anatomically separated from my well-developed implicit procedural and emotional impulse to "tell Marilyn about it" when I saw our books on the bookstore table.

These two kinds of memory can operate independently, almost unaware of each other, and can even be in conflict with each other. This view, my colleague stated, points to normal aspects of human behavior and memory, which we all rely on, and does not imply that my behavior is irrational. It would be odd indeed after sixty-five years of marriage if I did *not* have the impulse to tell her about our books when I see them even though I know she is gone.

———

Not everyone is *always* proud of his or her wife. But that was true for me, in spades. No matter the setting—I was always proud of her. I am so proud to have been her husband. I've *always* taken Marilyn's grace and knowledge as a given. I remember how wonderful she was in addressing a large crowd in an auditorium or speaking to a salon in our living room. She excelled, no matter the setting, no matter the competition.

She was a very good mother who loved her four children and always, always, was kind and generous to them. I have no recall in my entire life of a negative interaction between her and the children or, for that matter, anyone else. Was I ever bored or dissatisfied with our relationship? Never! I took it all for granted and never, until now, now that she is dead, have I so deeply appreciated how lucky I was to have spent my life with her.

Weeks have passed since her death and my longing for her is not diminished. I keep reminding myself that healing will be slow and that every single grieving patient I've seen has had to go through several unhappy months. But, I've never encountered a man and wife who were bonded at such an early age and were as close as we were.

I'm beginning to worry about my prognosis.

CHAPTER 27

NUMBNESS

NUMBNESS PERSISTS. My children visit. We take walks in the neighborhood, cook together, play chess, and watch movies on TV. Yet I remain numb. I feel uninvolved in the chess games with my sons. Winning or losing has lost significance.

Yesterday evening there was a neighborhood poker game, and my son Reid and I both played. It was the first time I've ever played together with one of my sons in a game of adults. I've always loved poker but at this game, at this time, I could not shuck the numbness. Sounds like depression, I know, but still I took pleasure in seeing Reid's happiness about winning thirty dollars. As I walked back to my home, I imagined how good it would have felt to arrive home, be greeted by Marilyn, and tell her about our son's winning night at poker.

The following night I try an experiment and place the portrait of Marilyn in plain view in the room while my son, his wife, and I watch a movie on TV. But, after a few minutes,

I feel so much tightness in my chest that I again put Marilyn's portrait out of sight. The numbness persists as the film proceeds. After about a half hour, I realize that Marilyn and I had seen this movie several months before. I lose interest in seeing it again, but remembering that Marilyn had enjoyed it a great deal, I honor the bizarre notion that I owe it to her to watch the entire film.

I notice that the numbness recedes the first few hours of the day when I am immersed in writing this book and also when I work as a therapist. Today, a woman in her late twenties enters my office for a consultation. She presents her dilemma. "I'm in love with two men, my husband and another man I've been involved with for the last year. I don't know which is the *real* love. When I'm with one of them, I feel that he's my *real* love. And then the next day or so I feel the same way about the other man. It's as though I want someone to tell me which one is the *real* love."

She discusses her dilemma at length. Midway through the session, she notes the time and mentions that she had seen my wife's obituary. She thanks me for being willing to see her at this difficult time. "I worry" she says, "about burdening you with *my* issues when you're suffering such a huge loss."

"Thank you for those words," I reply, "but some time has gone by, and I find that it helps me if I'm engaged in helping others. And also there are times when issues arising from my grief enable me to help others."

"How does that work?" she asks. "Are you thinking of something that may be helpful to me?"

"I'm not clear about that. Let me just ramble for a minute. Let's see . . . I know that getting involved in your life in this session temporarily diverts me from my own. I'm thinking, too, of your comment that you don't know your real self and that you cannot know which of these two men the *real* you *really* wants. I keep thinking about your use of *real*. I feel this may be tangential, but I'll just trust my instincts and tell you what our discussion stirs up in me.

"For a very long time I've felt that an event often felt 'real' only after I shared it with my wife. But now, weeks after my wife's death, I have this very strange experience of something happening and my feeling I must tell my wife about this. It's as though things don't become 'real' until my wife knows about them. And, of course, that is entirely irrational because my wife no longer exists. I don't know how to put this in a way that will be helpful but here it is: *I, and only I, have to take full responsibility for determining reality.* Tell me, does this have any meaning for you?"

She seems deep in thought and then looks up and says, "That *does* speak to me. You're right if you're implying that I cannot trust my sense of reality and that I want others—perhaps one of my two men, perhaps you—to identify *reality*. My husband is weak and always defers to *my* observations, to *my* sense of reality. And the other man is stronger, very successful in business, very sure of himself, and I feel safer and more protected and trust his sense of reality. Yet I also know that he's a long-term addict who is now in AA and has now been sober for only a few weeks. I think the truth is that I mustn't trust *either* of them to define reality for me. Your words make me realize that it's *my job to define reality—my job and my responsibility.*"

Toward the end of our hour together, I suggest that she is not ready to make a decision and should tackle this in depth in continued therapy. I give her the names of two excellent therapists and ask that she email me a few weeks from now to let me know how she is doing. She is deeply touched by my sharing so much with her and says that this hour has been so meaningful that she didn't want to leave.

CHAPTER 28

HELP FROM SCHOPENHAUER

I AM AWARE of the long dark time that lies ahead of me. In my many years of individual and group therapy work with bereaved individuals, I have learned that it is necessary for the patient to pass through all the year's major events for the first time without their spouse—birthdays, Christmas, Easter, New Year's, a first social outing as a single man or woman—before substantial improvement occurs. And for some patients even a second year, a second cycle, is necessary. When I look at my situation, especially at the length and the intensity of my bond with Marilyn, I know that I'm facing the darkest and most difficult year of my life.

My days pass slowly. Though my children and friends and colleagues make an effort to stay in touch, the number of visitors has slacked off, and I have now little desire or energy to reach out to others. Each day, after attending to incoming emails, I spend most of my time working on this book, and often I dread finishing it because I can think of nothing to replace it. Though I occasionally dine with a friend or one of my children, I eat more and more meals alone and spend evenings alone. Without fail, I end the day reading a novel. Recently, I started reading William Styron's *Sophie's Choice*, but after a couple of hours I realize that later sections of the book are going to be set in Auschwitz. Reading about the Holocaust just before going to sleep is the last thing I want to do.

I put aside *Sophie's Choice*, and while looking for another novel, I decide that perhaps it is time to reread some of my own books. I examine the bookcase where Marilyn had neatly placed all the books I had written. I pick up my four novels: *When Nietzsche Wept*, *The Schopenhauer Cure*, *Lying on the Couch*, and *The Spinoza Problem* and flip through their pages.

Oh, how I loved writing these books! The high point of my career! I try to recall how and where each of these books were born and written. The first memory to emerge took place on Silhouette, a small lovely island in the Seychelles, where I wrote the first chapters of *When Nietzsche Wept*. Then I recall when, after I lectured on group therapy in Amsterdam, Marilyn and I embarked on a long drive through Holland. After visiting Spinoza's library at Rijnsburg, we were heading back to Amsterdam when the entire plot of *The Spinoza Problem* floated into my mind.

I recall our visit to Schopenhauer's birthplace and his tomb and statue in Frankfurt, but realize that I could recall relatively little about *The Schopenhauer Cure*—far less so than the other novels I've written. I decide to reread it—the first time I have reread any of my novels.

As I start to read, my impressions are strong and, for the most part, positive. The novel is set in a therapy group, and what really catches my attention is the main character,

66-year-old Julius. He is the group therapist, described as
an old man who, having learned he has a fatal melanoma, is
looking back on his life. (Think about it: here I am, at the
age of 88, reading what I've written about *an old man of
66* facing death!)

The book has a dual focus: in alternating chapters I tell
the story of a therapy group and the life story of Schopenhauer who was both a wise man and a highly troubled one.
I describe a contemporary therapy group in which one of
the members, Philip, is a philosopher who not only teaches
Schopenhauer but very much resembles Schopenhauer in his
misanthropy. Hence the book not only informs the reader
about Schopenhauer's life and work, but also explores
whether Schopenhauer, a legendary pessimist and skeptic,
might have received help by a well-functioning contemporary therapy group.

Reading *The Schopenhauer Cure* is powerful therapy for
me. Page by page I grow calmer and more content with my
life. To my eye my sentences are well-composed, my word
choices good, and I believe I succeeded in engaging the
reader. How had I done it? The guy who wrote this book is
a hell of a lot smarter than I am and knows a lot more about
philosophy and psychotherapy than I do. And some of my
sentences take my breath away. Did I write that? Of course, as
I continue to read a few criticisms arise: for example, why did
I quote so many of Schopenhauer's anti-religious diatribes
in early chapters. Why go out of my way to shock religious
readers?

I am amazed to realize how much of this novel describes
my own life experience. I gave Julius, the group therapist,
many of my own attributes, as well as my own past. He, as

I, had had a difficult time with relationships early in life. Furthermore, he loved to gamble, and he ran the same type of baseball lottery I ran in high school. He even liked the same baseball players I adored—Joe DiMaggio and Mickey Mantle. To one of the women in the novel's therapy group, I gave my experience with Goenka, an eminent Vipassana teacher, in a ten-day retreat at Igatpuri, India. That part of the novel is entirely autobiographical and faithfully depicts a journey to India that left a deep impression on me. I cannot think of another such experience that remains in my memory with such clarity.

I prolong my rereading of the novel by rationing myself to only a single chapter each night just before turning off the light. Every night now, I look forward to the reading. My aging memory is, for the very first time, an asset: I recall so little of the book that the events of each chapter surprise and entertain me. It feels to me that the novel is a strong teaching guide that demonstrates how to recognize, clarify, and alter group members' interpersonal problems. As I recall, this was not one of Marilyn's favorite books because of my heavy emphasis on teaching group therapy. I also now remember that Molyn Leszcz, my good friend and co-writer of the fifth and sixth editions of my group therapy textbook, led an improvised dramatization of this particular therapy group with my son Ben and other members of his acting troupe for a large audience at an annual meeting of the American Group Therapy Association. What a delightful adventure that was!

As I continue my nightly reading, I am stunned to read, on page 238, these confessional lines spoken by Julius, the group leader, to the members of his therapy group:

I married Miriam, my high school sweetheart, while I was in medical school and ten years ago she was killed in a car crash in Mexico. To tell the truth, I'm not sure I've ever recovered from the horror of that event but to my surprise my grief took a bizarre turn; I experienced a tremendous surge of sexual energy.

At that time I didn't know that heightened sexuality is a common response to a confrontation with death. Since then I've seen many people in grief become suffused with sexual energy. I've spoken with men who've had catastrophic coronaries and tell me that they felt such powerful sexual urgings that they groped female attendants while careening to the ER in an ambulance.

This "surge of sexual energy" after the fictional Miriam's death and the observation that "many people in grief become suffused with sexual energy" that appear in my own book written almost twenty years ago predict the very things I've been experiencing after Marilyn's death and the very things I and my research assistants found, after considerable difficulty, in the psychotherapy literature. But this book, written at the time when I was leading therapy groups of bereaved spouses, had vanished from memory when the time came for me to deal with my own grief and my ensuing heightened sexual longings.

With each night's reading, I more fully appreciate that not only had I written an engrossing yarn that now offers me considerable help, but I had also written one of my best teaching guides for group therapists. I had intended this book to be a teaching novel—for both the beginning student in philosophy and for the student group therapist. I modeled a problematic patient, Philip, after Schopenhauer. Philip, a philosophy teacher specializing in Schopenhauer's work, had decided to switch fields and to become a philosophical counselor, and his training program required him to participate as a patient in a therapy group. Exactly like the real-life Schopenhauer, Philip was a schizoid, distant, isolated individual who had enormous difficulty both in accessing his feelings and in relating to others. Every time Philip was asked about his feelings, he denied having feelings. Julius, the group leader, regularly handled that beautifully by using one of my favorite ploys to help such patients work: he asked Philip, "If you *were* to have feelings about what just happened what *might* they have been?"

The novel continues to be read and has been translated into thirty languages. I try to remember where I was in the world when I wrote the novel. If Marilyn were alive, she'd tell me in an instant.

CHAPTER 29

DENIAL REVEALED

NINE WEEKS SINCE MARILYN DIED, and I've made little progress in dealing with my grief. If I were seeing me in therapy, I'd say Irv Yalom is significantly depressed. He is sluggish, feels numb, is despairing much of the time, losing weight, experiences little pleasure in life, is uncomfortable being alone, and overall, has made little progress in coming to terms with his wife's death. He says he knows that he is in for at least a year of feeling awful. He feels extraordinarily lonely. He knows it is essential to stay connected, yet he shows little initiative in seeking out the company of others. He gets little pleasure from anything and has no great desire to go on living. He has little appetite, warms up frozen dinners for meals, and mostly is indifferent to food. He has always loved watching tennis but recently watched only a couple of matches on TV from the Australian grand slam, and as soon as his favorite, Roger Federer, lost, he stopped watching. He knows very few of the younger players and takes very little interest in getting to know them.

So that's my objective observation of myself. I am, indeed, significantly depressed but not dangerously so. I do believe I will heal in tine. I've escorted a great many widows and widowers through these stages of despair and have some sense of what to expect. I'm not a suicide risk though I have no great fear of death. I most likely will die from a suddenly lethal coronary, and I must confess that, at this writing, there is a substantial part of me that would welcome it.

I'm currently reading a most interesting memoir of a bereaved husband, *The Widower's Notebook* by Jonathan Santlofer. I find much common ground with the author's experience. Several weeks after his wife's death (about where I am now), he has his first social outing in which he is unsettled by the many women who flirt with him. He realizes his good fortune: desirable widowers are rare, whereas there is always an abundance of widows. But he is confused: should he respond to women's sexual invitations? Would that not be a betrayal of his relationship with his departed wife? I identify very much with his dilemma and review in my mind all the women who have contacted me in the weeks since Marilyn died.

Marsha, a French scholar in her sixties and an old friend of Marilyn, invited me to dinner and we met at a nearby restaurant. Marilyn and I had often socialized with Marsha and her husband, and I was surprised (and a wee bit pleased) when she arrived alone at the restaurant. Her husband, I learned, was traveling to the East Coast. Our dinner conversation was extremely intimate, and she revealed much about herself that I had never known.

I had always liked and admired Marsha, an intelligent and extremely handsome woman, and during our dinner, I found myself admiring her more than ever and felt a bit—no, more than a bit—titillated by the many times she touched my hands during our dinner. I had taken an Uber to the restaurant because I no longer drive at night, and she insisted on driving me home even though it was the opposite direction for her. On our way home I felt aroused and struggled with the impulse to invite her into my home . . . and . . . and . . . and who knows what might happen? But, thank God, after a lively inner debate, I nixed that idea.

Later, as I lay in bed awaiting sleep and reviewing my evening's experience, a major insight thundered down upon me: "You identify readily with the widower Jonathan Santlofer's first excursion into the singles world, but, remember, *he is in his sixties.* Keep in mind that you are 88 *years old.* No woman, especially a happily married woman twenty-five years younger like Marsha, is going to come on to you—or to any man who such a short life expectancy. Since the beginning of time, no woman has been turned on by an 88-year-old man!"

Women obviously must realize I have only a short life span. At age 88, how much time do I have? Perhaps a year or two or three. Eighty-eight is extremely old in my family. My mother died at 90, but aside from her, I'm by far the longest living Yalom. Almost all my Yalom male ancestors died young. My father almost died of a severe coronary in his fifties but survived until age 69. His two brothers died in their mid-fifties. My balance is unstable. I walk with a cane and have an implanted metal pacemaker instructing my heart when to beat. And my belief that women in their sixties and seventies come on to me? Sheer delusion! I AM IN DENIAL. I am astounded by my naivete. And, of course, the force driving the denial is death anxiety—something I've explored and written about for so many years.

CHAPTER 30
STEPPING OUT

BIG CHANGES THIS WEEK! I attend an event every day
of the week! It was not that I initiated new things, but that
I accepted every invitation. I think that the real marker of
improvement will be when I start initiating events.

Monday begins with an email invitation:

Hello Everyone!

Please come to our next Barron Park Senior lunch on
Feb 11th at 1:00 pm

WHERE? Corner Bakery Cafe

3375 El Camino Real, Palo Alto

Order at the counter, request a 10% senior discount.

I have lived in this neighborhood almost sixty years and
have never received such an invitation, so I assume that this
is to be a gathering of widows and widowers. Through some

unknown mechanism, I have now been placed on this list. I'm generally too shy to attend such events by myself, but I am now officially alone so . . . well . . . why not? Perhaps it will be interesting. A senior lunch! There's no doubt I'm a senior. At 88 I'll probably be the most senior person there. I can't conceive of someone in their nineties attending such an event on their own.

I am a bit astonished by my decision to attend but think that perhaps it will lead to something worth writing about in this book. And it's likely to be better than yet again another Trader Joe's lunch by myself.

The Corner Bakery Café is only a few blocks from my home. There are about twenty people there—fifteen women and five men. Everyone is pleasant and welcomes me so warmly that I begin to feel comfortable after only a few minutes—more quickly than I had expected. Everything feels neighborly. The conversation is interesting, the food is good.

I'm glad to have gone, and most likely I'll attend next month's event. I assume I'll meet some of the attendees in my daily walks in the park a block from my home. It feels like a first step out into my new world.

Tuesday I meet with my regular men's group and, afterwards, Randy, one of the members and a good friend, drives me to the Stanford Book Store for a reading by the eminent Harvard psychiatrist and anthropologist Arthur Kleinman who speaks about his new book, *The Soul of Care*. Dr Kleinman speaks about "caring" (and the lack thereof in contemporary medicine), and his book describes his eight years of caring for his wife, who had a rare and ultimately fatal dementia. I loved his talk and his elegant and thoughtful answers to questions.

I purchase his book and joined the line for his autograph. When it is my turn, he asks my name. When I answer, he looks directly at me for a long time and writes these lines in my book: *"Irv, Thank you for the model of care you have been.—Arthur Kleinman"*

I am touched and proud. I had never met him before—that I can remember. He mentioned he had been a Stanford Medical School student from 1962 to 1966. Perhaps he had been in one of the classes I taught. I remember that I led many eight-session encounter groups for medical students the years he was a student. Perhaps I will email him and ask.

Wednesday I lunch with my colleague and good friend, David Spiegel, at the Stanford Faculty Club. I hadn't been there for at least a year during Marilyn's illness and had forgotten how pleasant a scene it is. Forty-five years ago, I heard David speak at a psychiatry conference and was so impressed by his keen mind and the scope of his knowledge that I facilitated his appointment to the Stanford psychiatric faculty. We've been very close friends these many years

Thursday I lunch again at the faculty club with Daniel Mason, a young member of our psychiatry faculty and a magnificent novelist as well. By error I arrive an hour early and walk to the Stanford Book Store a few minutes away. I experience great pleasure browsing through the new books. I feel like Rip Van Winkle waking up. That evening an old friend of ours, Mary Felstiner, comes over to my house for dinner, and we watch the Golden State Warrior's basketball game.

Friday I lunch with another friend.

Saturday I have my first hour with a trainer at the Stanford gym. My daughter, Eve, spends the evening.

Sunday, my son Reid joins me to play several games of chess.

This is by far the most active week I've had, and I'm aware that Marilyn has been less on my mind. As I write these words, I realize I hadn't looked at Marilyn's portrait the last couple of days, and I immediately stop writing. I walk the 120 feet from my office to my house to view Marilyn's portrait, which sits on the floor in the living room, still with its face to the wall. I pick it up and turn it around. I am staggered by her beauty. I imagine that I could walk into a room packed by a thousand women, and I would see no one but her.

So perhaps this week is portentous. I've tormented myself less. I've thought of Marilyn less often. *And, most importantly, I am ceasing to believe that she will know I'm thinking of her less often.*

I look at some notes I wrote only twenty days after Marilyn died:

On Friday the hospice social worker who works with bereavement will come to pay me a visit. Are there certain rituals that may help me that I haven't really taken advantage of? For example, Joan-Didion's book, *A Year of Living Magically* talks about a ritual of giving away clothes. I've engaged in none of these. I've been letting my daughter and daughters-in-laws take care of that, and I don't even know what's been done. I've just shut myself off from all this knowledge. Perhaps I should've participated in giving away her clothes and books and jewelry instead of avoiding everything having to do with the dead Marilyn. Again and again, I go into the living room and I stare deeply at Marilyn's portrait. Inevitably tears fill my eyes and run down my cheeks. I have a piercing feeling in my chest. Yet nothing has been accomplished. I'm drowning in the same torrent of pain. Why should I keep tormenting myself. What is so strange is the unreality of all of this. Marilyn keeps hovering in my mind. I can't quite make myself understand she is really dead. She no longer exists. Those words continue to stagger me.

As I read these words now, eighty-eight days after Marilyn died, I look at her picture and again feel overcome by her beauty. I want to hold her, to press her head to my chest, to kiss her. But there are fewer tears and no piercing wound, no torrent of pain. Yes, I know I shall never see her again. Yes, I know that death awaits me, that death awaits every living creature. Yet my death has not even entered my mind since Marilyn died. Though heaviness accompanies these thoughts: I am not overcome with dread. This is the nature of life and consciousness. I am grateful for what I have had.

CHAPTER 31

INDECISIVENESS

INDECISIVENESS IS SOMETHING I have in common with other widowers. I assiduously avoid making decisions. I've lived in Palo Alto for almost sixty years. For the past thirty years, I've also had a small apartment in San Francisco and would spend part of each week there. I would see patients there on Thursdays and Fridays. Marilyn would join me late Friday afternoon, and we'd spend the weekend together in San Francisco. But once Marilyn became ill, we never once made the hour-long trip to San Francisco, and my apartment has been vacant, aside from occasional use by one of my children.

Should I keep my San Francisco office and apartment? This question comes to mind often. Even now, three months after Marilyn's death, I have not left Palo Alto. I'm reluctant to go to San Francisco (or for that matter, anywhere). Somehow it feels as if the trip is more than I can manage. I no longer feel safe driving on the highway, though I could get there easily enough via Lyft or Uber or train. The apartment is at the top of a very big hill, and I'm doubtful that my loss of balance will permit me to walk up and down that hill. I try to imagine how I'd feel about going to San Francisco even if I had no balance problems, and I have a hunch that, if I had no problem walking, I'd still procrastinate. This is so uncharacteristic of me: I hardly recognize myself. I was always game for anything.

I worry about how costly it is to keep paying high condominium fees and taxes. But perhaps, I tell myself, those expenditures are offset by the apartment's appreciation in value. As is the case for most things, I put it out of mind—I avoid almost all decisions.

So, too, with automobiles. I have two cars in the garage, both five years old: my wife's Jaguar and my Lexus convertible. I know it's foolish to pay taxes and insurance on two cars that rarely get used. I've lost confidence in driving at night and now only use the cars in daylight to travel in my neighborhood to visit friends or go shopping. Perhaps I should sell both cars and buy a new one with more safety features, like a blind spot monitor that might have prevented a serious accident three years ago. I lunched the other day with two of my old poker chums. We had played in a game that lasted perhaps thirty years. One of them owns a dozen automobile agencies, and I asked him to check out my cars, make an offer, and suggest a new car for me. I'm hoping he will make the decision for me.

I've not been out to a play or concert or movie or to any event—aside from the Stanford bookstore reading—since Marilyn first got sick one year ago. I've always loved going to the theater. Recently, I heard about an interesting play being performed in a nearby community. I pushed myself to invite my daughter to go with me. But, by the time I had finished procrastinating, the play had finished its run. Other examples of such procrastination are numerous.

I receive an email showing the Stanford continuing education courses. There are two courses of great interest to me: "The Meaning of Life: Kierkegaard, Nietzsche and More" and "Masters of American Literature," the latter taught by a friend, Michael Krasny. Both sound wonderful. I wonder how I can get there at night. What if they are in buildings that are inaccessible by autos or require a long walk at night which is not possible for me? I tell myself that I will investigate it. But there's a fair chance I'll procrastinate and fail to attend either course.

It's as though I'm waiting for someone to rescue me. I feel like a helpless child. Perhaps I'm thinking magically—that my helplessness will somehow result in Marilyn's return. I'm by no means suicidal, but I believe I comprehend and empathize with the mentality of a suicidal individual as never before.

Suddenly I imagine someone, an old man sitting alone, watching a gorgeous glowing sunset. He is absorbed and entirely transported by the beauty surrounding him. Oh, I envy him. I wish to be like that man.

CHAPTER 32

ON READING MY OWN WORK

I BEGIN FEELING dark once again, and since reading *The Schopenhauer Cure* had been so helpful, I decide to read another one of my books. I check my bookshelf and, oddly enough, the book that seems most unfamiliar is one of my most recent ones, *Creatures of a Day*, a collection of psychotherapy tales published only five years ago. I follow the same reading pattern I had used earlier: only one chapter just before sleep each night. As before, reading my own work has considerable medicinal effect, and I want to prolong the reading as long as possible. With an introduction, an afterword, and twelve stories in the work, I look forward to enjoying relief from anxiety and depression for the next two weeks.

The blurbs on the front and back cover from eminent people whom I much respect strike me. I never thought this book contained my best work, yet these plaudits are the best I've ever received. As I read the third tale, "Arabesque," describing my interaction with Natasha, a colorful Russian ballerina, I am baffled that I cannot immediately recall her. At first I wonder if I had fictionalized a story about Sonia, a colorful Romanian ballerina, who was Marilyn's close friend. But, as the story proceeds, it is clear that Natasha was indeed a Russian ballerina whom I met with only three times and tried to help her recover from a lost love.

One passage near the end of the story particularly strikes me. As we approach the end of our meetings, I ask Natasha whether she has any questions for me.

She poses an audacious one: "How do you cope with being 80 and feeling the end approaching closer and closer?"

I answer: "A Schopenhauer observation comes to mind. He compares love's passion with the blinding sun. When it dims in later years, we become aware of the wondrous starry heaven that has been obscured by the sun."

On the next page, I read: "I treasure the pleasures of sheer awareness and I'm fortunate enough to share them with my wife whom I've known almost all my life." As I read these lines now, I realize once again that my task now is to treasure sheer awareness *on my own without Marilyn as witness.*

Though I remember my interaction with Natasha with much clarity, I keep straining to bring her face to mind, but it has entirely vanished from memory. For many years, I've harbored the notion that one is truly dead only when no living person can recall their face. For Marilyn and me, that would mean that we still persist as long as our youngest grandchildren live. Perhaps this is part of the reason for my sadness when I can no longer recall the face of a patient I knew long ago. It's as though I'm releasing someone's hand allowing them to drift off into oblivion.

Another story, "Thank You, Molly," begins at the funeral of my long-time personal assistant, Molly. I encounter Alvin, one of my patients, whom I had seen for a year of therapy. It turns out that he had also hired Molly to work for him. Molly worked for me for about ten years and her face is very clear in my mind, but I cannot see Alvin's face. The same is true for all ten of the stories. No faces appear to me even though the happenings of each story are very familiar, and the denouement appears in my mind long before I reach the end of each tale.

Also, in "Thank You, Molly," I am struck when I read a paragraph about Alvin's first encounter with death. Alvin's classmate in the seventh grade was an albino and had "large ears, bristle-brush white hair always standing at attention, bright brown eyes filled with wonder." He is absent from school for several days, and one morning the teacher informs the class that he has died of polio. I had given my character, Alvin, a part of my own past: in the seventh grade, I recall with great clarity, an albino boy named L. E. Powell who was the first person I knew who died. I find it extraordinary that I still, seventy-five years later, picture him in my mind's eye and still remember his name (though I barely knew him). I recall him eating cucumber sandwiches for lunch that his mother had made for him. I never heard of cucumber sandwiches before or since. I remember no other student from my seventh-grade class. Surely my memory recall of L. E. Powell issues from my early solitary struggle with the concept of death.

The seventh story has a catchy title: "You Must Give Up the Hope for a Better Past." It's not original, of course: the statement has been floating around for a long time. But I know of no other short phrase that carries such deep relevance for the process of therapy. I'm very moved by re-reading my story in which I work with a highly talented writer who, for a great many years, had buried her writing and her considerable talent.

I had forgotten much of the eighth story, "Get Your Own Damn Fatal Illness: Homage to Ellie," and rereading it was riveting. Ellie had metastatic cancer, and at the end of her first session she took a deep breath and asked, *"I wonder if you'd be willing to meet with me until I die?"* Ellie's story brings back to mind the many years in which I was haunted by death anxiety. Looking back, I'm struck by the fact that I worked so little on my dread in my own therapy. The topic never, not once, arose in my six hundred hours of analysis. Most likely my 80-year-old analyst, Olive Smith, was avoiding the topic herself. Twenty years later I began experiencing a great deal of death anxiety, as I started working with groups of patients with metastatic cancer and helping to escort many patients to their deaths. At that time, I began a course of therapy with Rollo May and focused a great deal on my death anxiety but never very successfully, even though Rollo always pressed me to go deeper. After he and I became close friends, years later, he told me that I had evoked much death anxiety in him during our therapy.

Ellie's cancer was aggressive, and I marveled at her ability to joust with death using an arsenal of denial-free ideas such as:

Life is temporary—always for everyone.
My work is to live until I die.
My work is to make peace with my body and to love it, whole and entire, so that from that stable core I can reach out with strength and generosity.

Maybe I can be a pioneer of dying for my friends and
   siblings.
I've decided to be a model for my children—a model
   of how to die.

Looking back I find her courage and the power of her
words to be breathtaking. I was not with her when she died:
I was on a three-month sabbatical in Hawaii writing a book.
I feel that I missed an extraordinary opportunity for a deeper
encounter with a great-souled woman. Now in the midst of
grief, I feel closer to my own death and find many of Ellie's
comments so highly relevant. Oh, how I wish I could revive
her by seeing her face in my mind once again!

CHAPTER 33

SEVEN ADVANCED LESSONS IN THE THERAPY OF GRIEF

FRIENDS KNOW that I'm always on the search for good novels. I've received many interesting suggestions recently, but, wishing to continue enjoying the therapeutic effects of reading my own books, I pick up *Momma and the Meaning of Life*, a book of stories I wrote twenty years ago and have not opened since. Thumbing through the table of contents, I am astonished, indeed shocked, to see the title of the fourth story, "Seven Advanced Lessons in the Therapy of Grief"! Ah, the travails of being 88 years old! How could I possibly have forgotten this story so pertinent to my current grief? It is, by far, the longest story in the book. I immediately begin reading. The first few lines trigger my memory, and the entire story bursts into mind.

I begin the story by describing a conversation with a close friend, a colleague in my department, who asks me to treat Irene, a friend and a surgeon on the Stanford faculty, whose husband had a malignant inoperable brain tumor. I very much wanted to be helpful to my friend, but taking on his friend as a patient felt sticky: I'd be involved in the kind of messy boundaries that every experienced therapist wishes to avoid. I hear alarm bells ringing, but wishing to be helpful to my friend, I turn the volume down low. Besides, the request was not unreasonable: at that particular time I was heavily engaged in research on the impact of group therapy on eighty bereaved spouses, and both my friend and I were convinced that few therapists knew more about bereavement than I. And there is one more persuasive point: Irene had told my friend that I was the only one smart enough to treat her—the perfect plug for my socket of vanity.

In our very first session, Irene immediately plunges into deep water and relates an astounding dream she had the night before our meeting: "My preparation for a course involves two different texts: an ancient and a modern text each with the same name. I am unprepared for the seminar because I haven't read either text. I especially haven't read the ancient first text which would have prepared me for the second."

"Do you recall the name of the texts?" I inquire.

"Of course" she answers immediately. "I remember clearly: each text was titled *The Death of Innocence.*"

This dream strikes me as "intellectual ambrosia," a gift from the Gods—an intellectual gumshoe's daydream come true. I venture a question: "You say the first text would have prepared you for the second. Do you have any hunches about the meaning of the texts?"

"Hardly a hunch! I know *exactly* what they mean."

I wait for her to continue. But she remains silent. I coax: "And the meaning of the texts is . . . ?"

"My brother's death at the age of twenty is the ancient text and my husband's death soon to come is the modern text."

We return many times to this "Death of Innocence" dream and her ensuing decision to avoid getting hurt by not letting others matter to her. Early in life she had decided to break off intimate relationships for that very reason. Eventually, however, she let herself care for a man, someone she had known since the fourth grade. She married him and now, far far too soon, he was dying. In the first session I got the clear message, via her curtness, her frosty manner, and her withholding information from me, that she had no intention of letting me matter to her.

After her husband died, several weeks after our first session, Irene relates another strong dream—the most vivid and eerie dream I have ever heard a patient describe: "I am in your office sitting in this chair but there is a wall in the middle of the room. I can't see you . . . I examine the wall: I see a small patch of red plaid fabric, then I recognize a hand, then a foot and knee. Suddenly I realize what it is: it is a wall of bodies heaped on one another."

"A red plaid patch, a wall of bodies between us, the, body parts—what do you make of that, Irene?" I ask.

"No mystery there . . . my husband died in red plaid pajamas . . . and here and now you cannot see me because of all the dead bodies, all of the deaths. You can't imagine. Nothing bad has ever happened to you."

In later sessions she adds that my life is unreal—"warm, cozy, always surrounded by your family . . . What can you *really* know about loss? Do you think you'd handle it any better? Suppose your wife or one of your children were to die right now. How would you do? Even that pink striped shirt of yours—I hate it. I hate what it says."

"What does it say?"

"It says, I've got all my problems solved. Tell me about yours."

Irene tells me about all of her acquaintances who have lost their spouse. "They all know that you never get over it . . . there's a silent underground who really know . . . all the survivors . . . the bereaved . . . you're asking me to detach from my husband . . . to turn toward life . . . it's all a mistake . . . a mistake of smugness from those like you who have never lost anyone . . ."

Such statements go on for weeks until, finally, she presses so many of my buttons that I lose it entirely. "So only the bereaved can help the bereaved?"

"Someone who has been through it," Irene calmly replies.

"I've been hearing that stuff ever since I entered the field," I shoot back to her. "And only addicts can treat addicts. Right? And do you have to have an eating disorder to treat anorexia? Or be depressed to treat depression? . . . And how about being schizophrenic to treat schizophrenia?"

Later I tell her about my research findings that show that every widow or widower gradually detaches from the dead spouse and that the spouses that had the best marriages went through the detachment process more easily than those with less fulfilling marriages who grieved for their squandered years.

Entirely unfazed by my comments, Irene calmly replies, "We bereaved have learned to give the answers you investigators want."

And so it continues for a great many months. We wrestle, we fight, but we stay engaged. Irene gradually improves, and early in our third year of therapy she met a man whom she grew to love and ultimately married.

CHAPTER 34

MY EDUCATION
CONTINUES

EARLY ON SATURDAY MORNING, I am awakened by severe pain in my neck. I get out of bed with an aching stiff
neck, the first time I have ever experienced such an affliction.
It persists for an entire week despite such treatments as neck
brace, pain medication, muscle relaxants, alternating hot and
cold compresses. Everyone at my age encounters bodily problems, but this is one of my very first encounters with such
persistent aggravating pain.

On Monday, I keep my long-scheduled appointment with
a neurologist who has been following me because of my balance problems. The most likely cause of the balance disorder
is a small bleed in my brain, but several X-rays have failed
to provide definitive evidence. In addition to my problems
with balance the neurologist focuses on some of the memory
problems I describe, and he gives me a fifteen-minute oral
and written test. I think I have done well, until he asks me,
"Now repeat those five items I asked you to remember." Not

only did I forget the five items, but I had forgotten that he had given me five items to recall.

He seems concerned with my performance and makes an appointment for me three months hence for a very thorough four-hour testing session at a neuropsychology clinic. There is nothing I fear more than severe dementia, and now that I live alone my fear of dementia has grown even worse. I'm unsure I want to be tested since there is no treatment available.

The neurologist also expresses concern about whether I should be continuing to drive. I don't like his saying this but, in part, I agree with him. I've been aware of my driving limitations: I am easily distracted, often I feel uncomfortable driving, and I no longer drive on the highway or at night. I had considered selling both my car and Marilyn's car and buying a new safer vehicle, but this meeting changes my mind. Persuaded that I'll not be driving for very long, I discard the idea of buying a new car. Instead I decide to sell Marilyn's car that she had loved for the past six years. I phone my friend who owns several car agencies, and he sent an employee to pick up Marilyn's car later that same day.

The following day I wear an uncomfortable neck brace, which I take off repeatedly to apply hot and cold compresses to my neck. I continue to think about my neurologist's concern about approaching dementia. But a far more disturbing event occurs when I walk outside and see my half empty garage, a garage no longer containing Marilyn's car. This opens up a rush of grief, and I think about Marilyn more this evening than I have for the past several weeks. I so much regret that I sold her car. Parting with it has ripped my grief wound open again.

This noxious cocktail—my body dealing with significant pain, impaired balance, insomnia resulting from my neck discomfort, the terror of failing memory, the vanishing of Marilyn's car—brings me to despair. For a couple of days, I sink into the deepest depression I have ever experienced. At rock bottom, I remain inert for hours, unable to do anything, not even grieve.

I just sit doing nothing, hardly aware of myself, for hours at a stretch. A friend is to pick me up to attend a Stanford Department of Psychiatry faculty dinner, but at the last moment I call him and cancel. I go to my desk and try to write, but no ideas come and I put away my writing. My appetite is poor, and I easily skip meals: I have lost about five pounds over the last few days. Now I more fully appreciate my earlier comments on the occurrence of sexual obsessions—*it is so much better to feel something rather than nothing*. Feeling nothing is an excellent description of my state of mind these last days. Fortunately Ben, my youngest son, arrives for a twenty-four-hour visit, and his energy and kindness enliven me.

After a few more days and some massages, the cervical pain subsides, and by the end of the week, I feel well enough to resume thinking and continue my work on this book.

———

As I look back on the weeks since Marilyn died, I realize I have had a remarkable postgraduate education. I have experienced firsthand three important conditions that so often challenge therapists.

First, there were the powerful obsessions that I could not halt: repetitive obsessive thoughts about the Tiananmen

Square massacre, and thoughts about women's breasts and about sexual encounters. All these obsessions have now faded, but I'll never forget my experience of powerlessness when I tried to stop them.

Then the experience of deep shattering grief. Though it is no longer searing, it still persists and is easily ignited by looking at Marilyn's portrait. I weep when I think of her. I write these lines on March 10, Marilyn's birthday, one hundred and ten days after her death.

And finally I've had a strong whiff of depression. I don't think I'll ever forget the experience of immobility, of deadness, of feeling inert and hopeless.

I now view my patient, Irene, through a different lens. Just as though it were yesterday, I recall so much of my encounter with her, particularly her comments about how my snug, cozy, fortunate life prevented me from fully grasping the devastation of her many loses. Now I take her words more seriously.

Irene, I believe you were right. "Smug and cozy" you called me—and you were correct. And if I were to see you now, now that I've lived through Marilyn's death, I am certain our work together would be different—and better. I can't specify what I would do or say, but I know I would experience you differently and that I would have found a more genuine and helpful way to be with you.

CHAPTER 35

DEAR MARILYN

My Dear Marilyn,

I know I'm breaking all the rules by writing you, but I've now come to the last pages of our book, and I cannot resist contacting you one last time. You were so wise to invite me to write this book with you . . . no, no, that's not right: you didn't *invite, you insisted that I put aside the book I had started and, instead, write this book together with you.* And I'll be forever grateful for your insistence—this writing project has kept me alive since you died one hundred twenty-five days ago.

Of course, you recall we wrote alternating chapters until two weeks before Thanksgiving when you grew too ill to continue and told me that I would have to finish the book on my own. I've been writing alone for four months—in fact, doing nothing but writing—and I'm now coming to the end. I've been circling around this last chapter for weeks, and now I know that I cannot finish it without reaching out to you one final time.

How much of what I've written and am about to write do you already know? With total assurance, my mature, scientific, rational mind says—*"zero, nothing, nada"*—whereas my child mind, my tender, weeping, lurching, emotional mind wants to hear you say, "I know everything, my darling Irv. I've been by your side, accompanying you every moment of your journey."

Marilyn, the first thing I must do is to address and shuck some troublesome guilt. *Forgive me, please, for not looking at your portrait more often.* I keep it in the sunroom but . . . to my shame . . . I keep it turned toward the wall!! I tried for a while to keep it face outward so I could look into your beautiful eyes every time I entered the room, but without exception, each time I looked at your picture, grief pierced my heart and I wept. Now, after four months, it's just beginning to ease. Now, for a few minutes almost every day, I turn your photo around and gaze into your eyes. The pain has lessened and now, once again, love-warmth flushes through me. Then I look at another photo of you I've just found. You are hugging me. My eyes are closed, and I am blissfully transported.

And I have yet another confession: I have not yet visited your grave! I haven't mustered the courage: the very thought of it evokes too much pain. But the children have all visited your grave each time they come to Palo Alto.

Since you last saw our book, I've written one hundred additional pages and am now working on these closing paragraphs. I found it impossible to change or eliminate a single word you had written, so I've asked Kate, our editor, to edit your chapters. At the end I describe your final weeks, days, even the moments when I was next to you, holding your hand, as you drew your last breath. Then I wrote about your funeral and all that's happened to me since.

I've gone through a deep abyss of grief—but how could it have been otherwise given that I've loved you since we were adolescents? Even now, as I think how blessed I was to have spent my life with you, I can't understand how it all happened. How was it that the smartest, most beautiful and popular girl at Roosevelt High School chose to spend her life with me? Me, the class nerd, the star of the chess team, the most socially awkward kid in the school! You loved France and French, and yet, as you often noted, I mispronounced every French word that ever came my way. You loved music and were such a beautiful, graceful dancer, whereas I am so tone deaf that my elementary school teachers asked me not to sing in class chorus exercises, and, as you well know, I was a disgrace on the dance floor. Yet you always told me that you loved me and saw great potential in me. How can I ever, ever, thank you enough? Tears pour down my cheeks as I type these lines.

The last four months without you have been the hardest months of my life. Despite innumerable calls and visits from our children and friends, I've been numb and depressed and felt very much alone. I was slowly recovering until three weeks ago when I sold your car. The following morning, I was crushed and overcome with despair when I saw the empty space in our garage. I've contacted an excellent therapist and have been seeing her weekly. She has helped considerably, and I'll continue working with her for a while.

Then, about a month ago, a coronavirus epidemic broke out, placing the entire world in jeopardy. It is unlike anything anyone of us has ever experienced, and at this very moment the US and almost all European countries, including France, are on a twenty-four-hour lockdown. It's extraordinary—all New Yorkers, Parisians, San Franciscans, Germans, Italians, Spaniards—most of the Western world—must stay isolated in their homes. All businesses, except for grocers and pharmacies, have been ordered to shut down. Can you imagine the huge Stanford Shopping Center closed? And the Champs-Élysées in Paris and Broadway in New York empty and shut down? It's happening at this very moment and it is spreading. Here is this morning's headline in the *New York Times*: "India, Day 1: World's Largest Lockdown Begins—About 1.3 billion Indians have been told to stay at home."

I know how you would have experienced this: you would have been weighed down with anxiety about me and our children and your friends throughout the world, and by all the daily reminders that our world is collapsing. I am thankful you didn't have to go through this: you followed Nietzsche's advice—you died at the right time!

Three weeks ago, at the very beginning of the epidemic, our daughter decided to move in with me for the interim. As you know, Eve is on the verge of retiring from Kaiser. When your children retire then you know you are truly old. Her gynecology department has made it possible for her to do all her doctoring online these last weeks. Eve has been a godsend. She is taking good care of me, and my anxiety and depression have faded. I think she saved my life. She is making sure that we're truly isolated and making physical contact with no one. When we take a walk in our park and pass folks on the path, we wear our face masks, as does everyone now, and we assiduously keep six feet away from anyone we pass. Yesterday, for the first time in a month, I got into the car. We

drove to Stanford and took a walk starting at the Humanities Center and walking to the Oval. It was entirely deserted
aside from a few other walkers all wearing face masks and all
keeping their distance. Everything is empty—the bookstore,
Tressider Student Union, the Faculty Club, the libraries.
Not a student in sight—the university is entirely shut down.

For the past three weeks, no one other than Eve or I
has entered our home, absolutely no one, not even Gloria,
our housekeeper. I will continue to pay Gloria until it is
safe for her to return. Same with the gardeners whom the
government has ordered to remain in their homes and not
to come to work. People my age are exceedingly vulnerable
and perhaps I may die of this virus but now, for the first time
since you left, I think I can say to you, "Don't worry about
me: I'm beginning to rejoin life once again." You're there,
with me, all the time.

So many times, Marilyn, I search my memory in vain—I
think of someone we met, some trip we took, some play we
saw, some restaurant we dined at—but all these happenings
have vanished from memory. Not only have I lost you, the
most precious person to me in the world, but so much of
my past has vanished with you. My prediction that, when
you left me, you would be taking with you a good part of
my past has proved to be true. For example, the other day I
recalled that we took a trip a few years ago to some isolated
location, and I remember that I brought *The Meditations
of Marcus Aurelius* with me, and to insure I would read the
entire book, I brought no other books with me. I remember
how I read and reread and relished every word. The other day
I tried, in vain, to recall *where* we had gone on that trip. Was
it an island? Mexico? Where? Of course it's not important,

but still it's troubling to think of such wonderful memories vanishing forever. Remember all those passages I read to you? Remember how I said that when you died you would take much of my past with you? Indeed, that has come to pass.

Another example: The other night I reread "The Hungarian Cat Curse," the final story in my book *Momma and the Meaning of Life*. You may recall that the main character of that story is a menacing talking Hungarian cat who is terrified as he approaches the end of his ninth, and final, life. It's the most fanciful and bizarre story I've ever written, and I have no idea where, in my life, in my memory, that story came from. What inspired it? Did it have anything to do with my Hungarian friend, Bob Berger? I imagine asking you about what inspired me to write this strange tale—after all, who else has ever written about a therapist working with a Hungarian talking cat? I am certain you'd remember precisely the source of this tale. So many times, Marilyn, I search my memory in vain: not only have I lost you, the most precious person in the world, but so much else of my world has vanished with you.

I feel certain that I'm approaching the end of my life and yet, strangely enough, I experience little anxiety about death—I'm having a freak bout of peace of mind. Now, whenever I think about death, the thought of "joining Marilyn" soothes me. Perhaps I shouldn't question a thought that offers so much balm, but I cannot escape my skepticism. After all, what on earth does *joining Marilyn* really mean?

Do you remember a conversation in which I expressed my wish to be buried side by side in the same coffin with you? You told me that in your years writing your book on American cemeteries, you never once heard of a coffin for two. That didn't matter to me: I told you I was greatly soothed by the thought of you and me in the same coffin, my body placed next to your bones, my skull next to your skull. Yes, yes, of course rational thought informs me that you and I won't be there—what remains is nonsentient, soulless, deteriorating flesh and bone. And yet the *idea, not the reality*, provides comfort. I, an ardent materialist, jettison my reason and bask unashamedly in the entirely fantastical thought that if you and I were in the same coffin, then we'd be together for all time.

Of course this is unreal. *Of course* I can never join you. You and I will no longer exist. It's a fairy tale! Since I was 13 I've never taken seriously any religious or spiritual views of an afterlife. And yet the fact that I, a devout skeptic and scientist, am, nonetheless, soothed by the thought of joining my dead wife, is evidence of the extraordinarily powerful desire we have for persistence and the dread we humans have of oblivion. I am left with renewed respect for the power and the soothing of magical thinking.

As I was writing these very last lines an extraordinary coincidence occurred: I received an email from a reader who had read my book *Becoming Myself.* His closing lines:

> But why, Dr Yalom, so much fear about death? The body dies, but consciousness is like a river, running through time . . . when death comes, then it's time to say goodbye to this world, to the human body, to the family . . . but it's not the end.

"It's not the end"—How much, how tightly, we humans, ever since the beginning of recorded history, have embraced and clung to this thought. Each one of us dreads death, and

each of us must find a way to cope with that dread. Marilyn, I so clearly remember your oft-repeated comment, "The death of an 87-year-old woman who has no regrets about her life is no tragedy." That concept—*the more fully you live your life, the less tragic is your death*—rings so very true for me.

Some of our favorite writers champion that viewpoint. Remember how Kazantzakis's life-loving Zorba urged: "*Leave death nothing but a burned-out castle*." And remember that passage by Sartre, in his autobiography, that you read to me: "I was going quietly to the end . . . certain that the last burst of my heart would be inscribed on the last page of my work and that death would be taking only a dead man."

I know that I will exist in ethereal form in the minds of those who have known me or read my work but, in a generation or two, anyone who has ever known the flesh-and-blood me will have vanished.

I shall end our book with the unforgettable opening words of Nabokov's autobiography, *Speak, Memory*: "The cradle rocks above an abyss, and common sense tells us that our existence is but a brief crack of light between two eternities of darkness." That image both staggers and calms. I lean back in my chair, close my eyes, and take comfort.

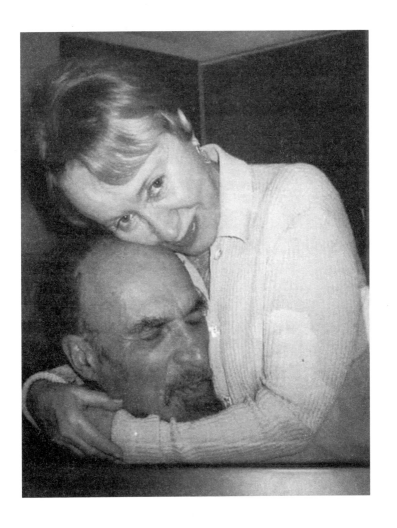